PHILIPPIANS

By LEHMAN STRAUSS

The First Person
The Second Person
The Third Person

Prophetic Mysteries Revealed
The Prophecies of Daniel
Devotional Studies in Galatians
        and Ephesians
James Your Brother
The Epistles of John
The Book of the Revelation

Certainties for Today
The Eleven Commandments
We Live Forever

Demons, Yes--but Thank God
        for Good Angels

Devotional Studies in

PHILIPPIANS

BY

LEHMAN STRAUSS

LOIZEAUX BROTHERS

Neptune, New Jersey

FIRST EDITION, SEPTEMBER 1959
SEVENTH PRINTING, JUNE 1982

ISBN 0-87213-823-2
PRINTED IN THE UNITED STATES OF AMERICA

PREFATORY NOTE

The messages in this little volume were originally prepared to be preached to the Sunday morning congregation of the Highland Park Baptist Church. The audiences who listened to them were most patient and have my warmest appreciation. I have thanked God many times for the obvious blessing upon the spoken Word in this series of sermons.

Without the aid of others, this book could not have been written. I am indebted to many authors for helps received from their writings, and to the following persons who gave of their time and strength in preparing the manuscript for publication—Miss Helen Hertzler, Mrs. Shirley Walter, and Mr. Samuel Scammon.

LEHMAN STRAUSS

Highland Park, Michigan

TABLE OF CONTENTS

7

I. INTRODUCTION

Philippi

The Philippian Epistle opens with an introduction to two men: namely, "Paul and Timotheos, the servants of Jesus Christ" (Phil. 1:1). At once our attention is directed to Acts, chapter 16, where we have the record of Paul's discovery of the young man Timothy. This beloved brother was destined to become the great apostle's faithful helper in the gospel. It is quite possible that Timothy was converted when Paul came to Lystra on his first missionary journey. In spite of the persecution in that place, Paul being stoned and left for dead (Acts 14:19), there was much fruit for his labor of love and sacrifice. God had saved a lad, half Jew and half Greek, thereby providing a fresh companion for His servant. Timothy joined Paul on the mighty apostle's return visit to confirm [i. e., to make firm, to strengthen] the churches (Acts 15:41), and he went with Paul and assisted in founding the local assembly at Philippi.

Philippi was a town of Macedonia in the northern area of the Aegean Sea. The city was named after Philip, king of Macedonia and father of Alexander the Great. It had any number of natural advantages with rich deposits of gold and silver, in addition to its fertile plains, well watered by the Gangites. Geographically it was a strategic

11

point, "commanding the great high road between Europe and Asia" (J. B. Lightfoot).

The gospel was first preached at Philippi by the Apostle Paul on his second missionary journey about the year 52 or 53. In addition to Paul and Timothy, the crusade team was made up of Silas (Acts 15:40), and Luke the physician who wrote the account in Acts. It is possible that Luke was brought into contact with Paul in a medical capacity. The commencement of the "we" section is in Acts 16:11, where Luke the author appears for the first time.

The practical lessons to be learned from Paul's visit to Philippi are too numerous to be taken up at this point. We will limit ourselves to three.

A. *The Voice of the Spirit*

After ministering the Word in the province of Galatia, Paul and his associates were minded to continue their crusade for Christ throughout Asia, but God had different plans for them. Luke says that they "were forbidden of the Holy Ghost to preach the Word in Asia" (Acts 16:6). When, as a young Christian, I first read these words, I could hardly believe my eyes. Had I read correctly, "forbidden to preach"? Yes, exactly that! Both the "steps" and the "stops" of good men are ordered of the Lord and He delights in both. It is possible to keep on going and serve as we go, yet not be in the place of God's appointment. Sometimes the Spirit restrains before He constrains. It is important that the place in which we serve should be by divine appointment. We dare not choose our location for service on terms other than those set forth by the Holy

Spirit. "They assayed to go into Bithynia: but the Spirit suffered them not" (Acts 16:7).

The Spirit may prevail upon us to go or He may prevent our going. We need spiritual perception and sensitivity to hear the Spirit's voice. "*He* that hath an ear, let *him* hear what the Spirit saith unto the churches" (Rev. 2:7, 11, 17, 29; 3:6, 13, 22). When we are divinely directed, there is evidence of a right relation to God; "For as many as are led by the Spirit of God, they are the sons of God" (Romans 8:14).

There is far more reward in obedient witnessing to one than in preaching out of the will of God to thousands. It may be that the Spirit will direct us to witness to one lonely individual as He did Philip. This servant of God was preaching to great crowds in Samaria with apparent success, but "the Spirit said unto Philip, Go near, and join thyself to this chariot" (Acts 8:29). I am not surprised at the Spirit's speaking to Philip, but I rejoice in Philip's recognizing the Spirit and his ready response to obey. We need the leading the early Church experienced when, "as they ministered to the Lord, and fasted, the Holy Ghost said, Separate me Barnabas and Saul for the work whereunto I have called them" (Acts 13:2).

The Holy Spirit both selected His servants in the early days of the churches and directed them. The tremendous success they enjoyed lay in their willingness to be led. When we are ready and willing to place ourselves at the disposal and direction of the Holy Spirit, we may be sure that He will lead and guide us into definite spheres of activity where no power will be able to resist Him. These servants would feel lost in the maze of modern methods and ecclesiastical machinery, but their ministry bore the stamp of divine hands.

Not one of us can afford to miss the Spirit's voice as He seeks to direct our way. If we forego divine direction, we will end the journey of life fruitless and frustrated. Human reasoning may make us feel as though we should push on in a given direction, but even though everything visible to the eyes and rational to the mind may seem natural and proper, we must watch for God's "stop" sign. The Holy Spirit is the Regulator of our lives, and in this highly specialized ministry He is both the propelling and restraining Force. His "no" is just as important as His "go." God has a place and a part for each of His children, and we should make certain that we are not practicing our vocation in the wrong location. Oh, for more Christians who will follow the Spirit's forbidding as well as His order to advance!

Paul and Silas were not moving aimlessly about looking for openings to hold meetings. Their well-mapped-out missionary program was orderly and had as its ultimate goal the salvation of souls and the establishing of young believers in the faith. Yet this sincere effort was halted by divine intervention. On the one hand they were *forbidden;* on the other they were *bidden.*

God may *dispose* of the very thing that an honest servant of His will *proposes*. This incident in the lives of Paul and Timothy illustrates this.

Adoniram Judson set out to give his life to preaching the gospel in India; but when he arrived at an Indian mission station, God forbade him to complete his mission. Instead, the same Voice from Heaven bade him go to Burma. Judson obeyed the bidding of God, and the results are with us to this day. Adoniram Judson and his lovely wife, Ann, have left us the record of a most thrilling accomplishment for Jesus Christ among the Burmese. Read the account of this in *The Splendor of God*.

He who misses divine direction reduces his spiritual stature and fails to be his best for God. No doubt there are Christians struggling along with a second or a third choice simply because they missed God's first and best choice for their lives. Make certain that you are faithful to the leading of God's Spirit and watch always for His restraining influence.

There is a dearth today of the knowledge of the will of God in Christian service. Not a few Christians graduate from Bible schools, colleges, and seminaries with a knowledge of what the textbooks say and the stand their institutions take on a certain doctrine or evangelist, yet they are ignorant of how to know the will of God for their own lives.

Paul found God's will by communing with God's Spirit. Be sure you find it, too.

B. *The Vision of the Sinner*

After the voice of the Holy Spirit came the vision of a lost sinner. "There stood a man of Macedonia, and prayed him, saying, Come over into Macedonia, and help us. And after he had seen the vision, immediately we endeavored to go into Macedonia, assuredly gathering that the Lord had called us for to preach the gospel unto them" (Acts 16:9-10).

There has been much speculation as to just who the man of Macedonia was. Some guess it was Luke; others conjecture that it was the Lord Jesus Himself. The Bible does not say; therefore any attempt to identify him is to say more than the Bible says. We do not know who he was. Suffice it to say that Paul saw in the vision another step in the course of events indicating the leading of the Spirit.

Such a momentous decision to leave Asia Minor and board a vessel for Europe called for a clear revelation from God. As far as Paul knew, this was it. The populated cities of Europe needed the gospel. Paul arose to the occasion to meet that need.

The cry, "Help us," implies that heathenism has no workable self-redemptive plan, and certainly no self-redemptive power. With all of its brilliant civilization and culture, it needed what Christianity alone could supply.

Luke says: "*Immediately* we endeavoured to go into Macedonia." Straightway, with alacrity, the new opportunity to serve God in the place of His choosing was seized. Our great American cities with their teeming population, their boasted scientific and industrial progress, and their advancements and achievements in education are calling, "Come and help us curb the rising tides of juvenile delinquency, divorce, murder, dope addiction, obscene stories and pictures, and corruption in labor unions." There is a Macedonia for each of us wherever we are, and the cry from human hearts is for the help the Christian gospel alone can give. A vision of lost sinners constitutes the "Macedonian call" to every Christian. Will we help those needy ones enroute to hell?

It is just such a vision that impels all true men and women of Christ to carry the gospel to every creature. But don't look for a man in a night vision—neither a Chinese, a Japanese, a Burmese, a Latin-American, nor a

European! The vision is a clear and indelible one, eternally and indestructibly inscribed by God the Holy Spirit. It is written: "But ye shall receive power, after that the Holy Ghost is come upon you: and ye shall be witnesses unto Me both in Jerusalem, and in all Judaea, and in Samaria, and unto the uttermost part of the earth" (Acts 1:8). There you have it! Every soul has a right to hear the gospel of Jesus Christ, and every Christian is committed to the task of disseminating this good news of salvation. That is your vision and mine. Do we see it clearly, or has our vision been made dim by the dazzling attractions of this world system?

Paul, and his companions in the gospel, could do nothing other than obey God, so "from thence to Philippi" (Acts 16:12). If we had nothing more to tell of their visit to that Roman colony, we would expect to hear sometime, somewhere, of a good work for God in the city of Philippi. And so we shall! God's obedient servants cannot be stopped nor stymied by what the enemies of the gospel can say or do against them. Europe heard the gospel of Jesus Christ because Paul obeyed the Spirit's voice more than nineteen hundred years ago. As he went he could not foretell the results, but he was assured that he went in the will of the Lord. Are *you* just as certain that *you* are serving your Lord faithfully in His divinely chosen place? I trust so!

This brings us to our third and final thought in this introductory chapter:

C. *The Victory of the Saviour*

God is no man's debtor. Response to the divine call and the human cry for help is bound to reap rich results.

Paul obeyed the voice and the vision, and the outcome was victorious and glorious. He answered the call of God and witnessed Jesus Christ and His gospel triumph over pagan idolatry and satanic opposition.

The beginning of the gospel in Philippi was an insignificant one and one of quiet waiting for the Lord to move. It started on a small scale. There was no planned crusade preceded by an "advance man," no publicity committee, no "kick-off banquet," no appeals to the local churches to cooperate. Paul's ministry in Macedonia was New Testament evangelism at its best. As he and his little party stepped off the vessel, there was no anxious group waiting to receive him, no transportation arranged to carry him to a hotel. How fine had someone been there to greet him, and say, "We welcome you, Brother Paul, and we are anxious to hear the message God will give through you." But there was nothing like that. Luke merely states: "We were in that city abiding certain days" (Acts 16:12). That is, they were waiting for the Spirit of God to make possible their first contact for Jesus Christ.

Young people, heed the lesson here, and you will be spared the disappointment and defeat that many have experienced upon arriving on the mission field. When you answer the call of God to go to some faraway place to take the gospel, do not be surprised to discover that nobody wants you. The need will be there, but remember, the heathen in most instances do not know their need. It is not until after they hear the Word of God that they are brought to see their need. But the fact that they have the need is the call for you and me to go and help them.

The day Paul and Luke and Timothy and Silas arrived in that Roman colony, little did the Roman powers know that this little band of missionaries were soldiers of the unconquered Christ and that, on that very day, these missionaries were raising the blood-stained banner of the Cross on Rome's frontal stronghold. The sowing of the gospel seed in that great center of world government was to change the course of history. The victories won by the forces of Jesus Christ, under the direct leading of the Holy Spirit, were proof enough that Satan is no match for the Son of God.

The first victory of the Saviour was in the conversion of just one woman.

After Paul and his companion had rested and quietly observed during the first few days, they set out on the Sabbath day for the place of prayer. This tells us that there was no synagogue in Philippi, for it was the custom of the Jews that if ten men could be gathered, that would be sufficient to start a synagogue. If not, then those who wished to worship would gather near some body of water where they could avail themselves of ceremonial rites which the stream provided.

Upon arriving at the riverside, Paul found a small group of women who had gathered to offer prayers. This, he concluded, was his opportunity, given by God, to bear witness to the power of Christ's saving gospel.

What prospects could a great preacher find in so unpretentious an audience made up of a few women? Knowing that his mission was ordered of the Lord, Paul could not be indifferent to their spiritual needs. He was appreciative of the few who were ready and receptive to the Word of God. One of that group was Lydia, a businesswoman, who sold dyed materials. She had come from Thyatira, a leading city of Asia. The Spirit had restrained Paul from going to Asia, but He had an openhearted woman from Asia waiting to receive the gospel. How blessed! "When He putteth forth His own sheep, He goeth before them. . . ." (John 10:4) The Lord had opened her heart; that is, He had prepared this woman, for "she attended unto the things which were spoken of Paul" (Acts 16:14). The open and obedient heart of one person to the truth of God is sufficient vantage ground to establish a base for the gospel of Jesus Christ. Lydia led her household to Christ and all were baptized (Acts 16:15).

There are some suggested evidences that this woman was truly saved. First, the Lord Himself had opened her heart. Although she had a religious profession, her heart was shut to the truth of the gospel. T. Walker says the word "opened" is a compound verb, and suggests the thought of "completely opened." There was no half-hearted reception of the truth here! God was in this, and He alone can completely open our ears to hear (Mark 7:34-35), our eyes to see (Luke 24:31), our minds to understand (Luke 24:44-45), our hearts to experience (Acts 16:14), and the Scriptures in order that we might know (Luke 24:32). We need the power of the Holy Spirit to break through the pride and prejudice of our hearts and to open them completely to the whole of God's Word. Too many today believe a half-truth or have but a smattering of the truth.

Secondly, when the Lord opened Lydia's heart, "she attended unto the things which were spoken of Paul"; that is, she was teachable. The blessed truths of the gospel were new to her but she grasped them eagerly. It was so with the new converts on the Day of Pentecost. Luke says: "They continued stedfastly in the apostle's doctrine [i.e., teaching]" (Acts 2:42).

It is a mark of genuine conversion when those who confess Christ with their lips continue in search of the truths of the Bible. The extent of our quest to know and obey the Word of God will determine, to a large extent, our spiritual development. We must give diligence to add "knowledge" to our "faith" (2 Peter 1:5). We must follow on to know, and we can grow only as we know (2 Peter 3:18).

The second victory won by our Lord through Paul proved the power of God over the power of Satan. In the city there was a certain young woman possessed of an evil spirit of divination. The margin says "a spirit, a Python." According to Greek mythology, Python was the name of a great dragon at Delphi which had been slain. Apollo was said to have slain the dragon, and, in consequence, he received the title "Pythius," and with the title the dragon's oracular power. Actually, the girl was demon-possessed and no doubt was gifted with clairvoyance and the power to make certain predictions. She was the property of certain men who formed a syndicate to make money from her gifts. Actually, Satan was the one who possessed this young woman, and when he saw that the gospel was commencing to Christianize Europe, he decided at once to use her in order to hinder God's servants.

Notice the satanic strategy. The young woman followed Paul and his associates and shouted: "These men are the servants of the most high God, which shew unto us the way of salvation" (Acts 16:17). At first glance it might appear as though she was aiding Christ's witnesses. Actually, Satan's strategy was to associate her with God's servants in the minds of the people. If the devil can associate a preacher or a missionary or any one of God's children with anything wrong or worldly, he can cripple their influence for God. What she said about Paul, Silas, Timothy, and Luke was true, but the whole plot was intended to defeat the gospel. In the devil's hand the truth can throttle the Church's power. Mark 5:1-8 illustrates this very idea.

But remember, Paul is where he is by the direct leading of the Holy Spirit. God had sent him to Europe; therefore God will safeguard His interests there.

Paul, turning from his friends and followers, said to the demon: "I command thee in the name of Jesus Christ to come out of her. And he came out the same hour" (Acts 16:18). No demon can withstand the power of our Saviour's Name. Later on Paul wrote: "But thanks be to God, which giveth us the victory through our Lord Jesus Christ" (1 Cor. 15:57), and again, "Now thanks be unto God, which always causeth us to triumph in Christ" (2 Cor. 2:14).

G. Campbell Morgan calls this experience the hour of gravest peril for the gospel in Philippi, the hour when Satan told the truth. Paul refused the patronage of hell even when it attempted to speak the truth about Christ. Let us beware of any alliance with evil, even when the evil tells the truth. Our only hope for victory is close by the Holy Spirit's leading, lest we be deceived.

Unable to hinder the gospel through an attempted alliance, Satan now attacks with opposition. When the syndicate owners saw the hope of their getting rich was gone, they became angry and brought charges against the Christians (Acts 16:19-21). They accused Christ's witnesses of teaching customs not consistent with Roman law. In reality they cared nothing about the law. They cared only about the money they might lose.

Touch some men's pocketbooks and you touch their god. Men and women today who peddle their poison wares are enemies of the gospel. Those who make their money through prostitution, gambling, liquor, obscenity, and the like are bitter antagonists of the gospel of Jesus Christ. And there is no end to which they might not go to silence a witness for Christ. In Philippi they put Paul and Silas in prison after beating them unmercifully (Acts 16:22-24). It would seem as though Luke and Timothy escaped.

For the time, it appeared that the gospel was not triumphant, but this was only momentary. No doubt Paul and Silas, their backs bleeding and their bodies shot through with pain, might have wondered if it were profitable to be so outspoken for Christ. I wonder if either was tempted to ask the other if he should not have gone into Asia. I wonder if they raised the question in their minds as to the possibility of making a wrong choice when coming to Philippi. Let us see! "And at midnight Paul and Silas prayed, and sang praises unto God: and the prisoners heard them" (Acts 16:25).

The religion of most people does not work in time of trouble. Christianity alone makes a man content, regardless of his state and circumstances (Phil. 4:11). Anybody can sing when life is full of prosperity, good health, and laughter, but it takes a spiritual Christian, who is certain that he is in God's will, to rejoice and praise God in the midst of trouble.

The attitude and action of Paul and Silas tell us at once what their relationship was with God. Imagine those beaten prisoners praying and praising God! They were suffering as a Christian ought to suffer. Not merely were they "called Christian" (Acts 11:26) nor merely were they "almost" persuaded to be Christian (Acts 26:28), but they *were* Christian, for they suffered as Christians and were not ashamed as they glorified God in their trouble (1 Peter 4:16). They were glorifying God in their bodies, for their bodies belonged to God (1 Cor. 6:20). Christian, be careful how you suffer. The gospel of Christ saves from the penalty and power of sin, but it likewise saves the believer from defeat and bitterness in times of difficult circumstances.

About eight or nine years after this prison experience at Philippi, Paul wrote: "And we know that all things work together for good to them that love God, to them who are the called according to His purpose" (Rom. 8:28). Now apply the principle in this verse to Paul and Silas in prison. Something is bound to happen, and it must be "good." And that good thing did happen. A miracle took place. "Suddenly there was a great earthquake, so that the foundations of the prison were shaken: and immediately all the doors were opened, and every one's bands were loosed" (Acts 16:26).

I do not question Satan's power to cause an earthquake, but he certainly did not cause this one nor could he prevent it. God did it, and He did it for "good" because two of His suffering servants loved Him. Peter experienced a similar deliverance from prison when God miraculously loosed Peter's chains and the locks on the prison gates (Acts 12:5-11).

The earthquake awakened the jailer, and in dismay and much distress he drew his sword, his first thought being of suicide: he supposed the prisoners, for whom he was responsible, had fled. Paul called loudly to him, appealing to him not to take his life. No man has a right to take his own life, for suicide not only brings harm to the man who kills himself, but to others as well. Suicide never solved anyone's problems.

Life's most vital question and God's only answer were soon to become apparent. Hearing Paul's voice, the jailer no doubt recognized it as coming from one who, a little while before the jailer fell asleep, was praying and praising God. That singing and praying had borne a good witness for Jesus Christ and His gospel. Then, trembling, he fell on his knees before Paul and Silas, and said: "Sirs, what must I do to be saved?" (Acts 16:30) Paul's answer was brief and to the point. There was no attempt at explaining the nature of the ordinances, no going into a discussion of Christian doctrine. Immediately they said: "Believe on the Lord Jesus Christ, and thou shalt be saved, and thy house" (Acts 16:31). He believed at once and was saved that very moment.

The proof of his conversion is seen in his actions. Earlier in the day he took delight in beating God's servants; now he is washing their wounds. When a man seeks to straighten up the past and make right his wrongs, it is a sign he means business with God. Then the jailer took these men home and fed them. Now that he was saved, the love of Christ constrained him to do something for God and His servants.

The gospel continued to work through the jailer, and his entire family believed on the Lord Jesus Christ. They were baptized in obedience to the divine command (Matt. 28:19; Mark 16:16; Acts 2:38; 8:36-39; 9:17-18; etc., etc.). It is quite likely they formed a part of the local assembly in Philippi to whom Paul wrote the letter we are about to study together.

The victories won at Philippi in the name of our Lord Jesus Christ are eternally and indelibly written for our instruction and encouragement. Not even the gates of hell can prevail against the power of the Christian gospel. Give us men and women, led by the Holy Spirit, who will remain steadfast under provocation, and we too shall see the victory as did God's servants in Europe.

II. PRELUDE

Paul and Timotheus, the servants of Jesus Christ, to all the saints in Christ Jesus which are at Philippi, with the bishops and deacons:

Grace be unto you, and peace, from God our Father, and from the Lord Jesus Christ.

Philippians 1:1-2

A. *The Servant*

The introduction to the Philippian Epistle, like that in Paul's letters to the Romans (Rom. 1:1) and to Titus (Titus 1:1), introduces the writer not as an apostle but as a "servant of Jesus Christ." Here Timotheus (Timothy) is included, so the text reads: "the servants of Jesus Christ."

Timotheus, or Timothy, needed no introduction to the Philippians. He had accompanied Paul and Silas when the church was founded, and at that time he "was well reported of by the brethren" (Acts 16:2). During those intervening years between the founding of the church and the writing of this Epistle, Timothy had possibly visited the brethren at Philippi, so that the appearance of his name in the salutation would seem quite natural to the readers there.

The word "servants" conveys the thought of bond-slaves, the purchased property of Jesus Christ. This kind of servitude carries with it no attractive array of authority. Actually, Paul was Caesar's prisoner in Rome, but

27

he considered himself to be the prisoner of the Lord. Four times in this first chapter he refers to his "bonds" (verses 7, 13, 14, 16), not in bitter complaint but rather as a blessed bondage. The occasion of his imprisonment in Rome was his preaching of the gospel, yet we find no trace of despair or despondency, only words of joy and good cheer. The apostle had come to Philippi in response to the Spirit's leading, and now his prison experience in Rome he considers no less the will of God.

The word "servant" is *doulos,* and it refers to one who is bound to another. Into this sweet servitude Paul came by way of the new birth. When he was apprehended by the Lord Jesus Christ, Paul surrendered at once to a new Master when he said: *"Lord,* what wilt Thou have me to do?" (Acts 9:6) Paul's will was swallowed up by the sweet will of Jesus Christ, and if Christ willed that His servant sit in a prison cell, then in such a state that servant will be content. And why not? God is not cut off from His children by a wall. Many wonderful works were produced behind prison walls, such as Cervantes' *Don Quixote,* Marco Polo's *Travels,* and Bunyan's *Pilgrim's Progress.* Thank God for those jails and prisons that have brought forth those literary classics. Sitting bound in prison, Paul saw in a figure his own relation to Jesus Christ, that of a bondslave, and he gloried in it. A wrong attitude on Paul's part never would have produced this Epistle of joy.

This humble, self-appellation, "servants of Christ," describes the true position of all the redeemed. Every believer is the purchased possession of the Saviour, and when Christ takes control, self-esteem and self-importance are renounced. All workers of the Lord surrender unconditionally for service under their new Master, for it is honor and authority enough to be allowed by Jesus Christ to be His servants.

Service was the sum and substance, the ultimate of Paul's whole life, for this was his conception of the Christian life. He followed hard to lay hold of that for which Christ had laid hold of him (Phil. 3:12). Paul did not merely express his views in a letter; he expended his vitality in labor. Too many do little more than testify with their lips as to when and how they found Christ. They have neither stopped nor studied to think what actually took place in their lives. Christ was never lost; we were lost, helplessly lost, and He found us. He Himself said: "Ye have not chosen Me, but I have chosen you, and ordained you, that ye should go and bring forth fruit, and that your fruit should remain: that whatsoever ye shall ask of the Father in My name, He may give it you" (John 15:16).

We need more men and women in the church who are ready and willing to write after their names, "servants of Jesus Christ," and then go out to make good their witness. There is too much of the spirit of James and John, whose ambition was to be chiefest in Christ's Kingdom, and not enough of the example of Christ Himself, who said: "I am among you as He that serveth" (Luke 22:27). When Paul wrote of Him who "took upon Him the form of a servant" (Phil. 2:7), he was following his Lord.

Any Christian who makes himself subservient to Jesus Christ will find in his Lord both the sufficiency (Phil. 4:13), and the supply (Phil. 4:14) for service. And permit me to add that no believer can know true freedom in everyday experience who does not surrender to the mastery and lordship of Jesus Christ. James who, by the Holy

Spirit, wrote: "Faith without works is dead" (James 2:20, 26), considered himself "a servant of God and of the Lord Jesus Christ" (James 1:1). This is the only servitude I know anything about with sweetness in it. It is, in the fullest sense of the word, a bondage of blessing. May God draw us, by divine grace and power, to enter in to enjoy it to the full.

"Know ye not, that to whom ye yield yourselves servants to obey, his servants ye are to whom ye obey; whether of sin unto death, or of obedience unto righteousness? But God be thanked, that ye were the servants of sin, but ye have obeyed from the heart that form of doctrine which was delivered you. Being then made free from sin, ye became the servants of righteousness. I speak after the manner of men because of the infirmity of your flesh: for as ye have yielded your members servants to uncleanness and to iniquity unto iniquity; even so now yield your members servants to righteousness unto holiness" (Rom. 6:16-19).

B. *The Saints*

All Christians are "saints" as well as "servants," and in an unmistakably clear statement, Paul addresses himself "to all the *saints* [literally, *the holy ones*] in Christ Jesus which are at Philippi, with the bishops and deacons" (Phil. 1:1).

Is there any significance in the fact that Paul places the saints before the oversight brethren in the local assembly? I do not know. However, I could not help but notice the order. The overseers are not to be lords over God's heritage but sharers in their joys and needs. As a pastor, I am convinced that none in our local assembly are more important than the saints. If you wonder why I say this, I can only answer that the saints make up the church, for without them there would be no church.

But to whom is Paul referring by the use of the word "saints"? This is one of God's names for His own. The term nowhere in the New Testament is reserved for any who attain to exceptional holiness in character. Nor is it ever reserved for those in Heaven now who were saintly on earth. Its simple meaning is "set apart," and it applies to all true believers in the Lord Jesus Christ. All God's people are thus designated, regardless of the proportion of spirituality to which they might have attained. The blood of Jesus Christ is upon them and marks them as a positionally set-apart, consecrated, holy people.

There is something about this word "saint" that reminds me of the sacred nature of *my* position in Christ: namely, I am God's set-apart property, just as every believer in Jesus Christ is. The expression "all the saints," does not exclude any believer in Jesus Christ, and certainly it obliterates any distinction between classes of Christians.

Paul did not call them saints because they were perfect people. Quite the contrary! There was an imperfection in the assembly, and Paul dealt with it when he said: "I beseech Euodias, and beseech Syntyche, that they be of the same mind in the Lord" (Phil. 4:2).

A saint belongs to God but he is not perfect. There are many particulars in the lives of the saints that might be improved upon. Saintliness, in its perfection, is the final achievement of Christ for His own, and it can never be realized until He comes again, for ". . . we know that, when He shall appear, we shall be like Him; for we shall see Him as He is" (1 John 3:2).

Holy people may be at times unholy people in this life. Saints are at times unsaintly. However, the goal will be realized when the practical process of sanctification is perfected (2 Cor. 3:18).

Now I have not overlooked the practical requirements of our position as saints. We who are *positionally* holy are required to be *practically* holy. We see both this positional relationship and the practical requirements in the Epistle to the Ephesians. Paul addresses the believers as "saints" (Eph. 5:3). In other words, be what you are. Be in practice what you are in position. Be in behavior what you are in belief.

Guy H. King points out in the English Bible Paul's salutation in Romans and First Corinthians. It reads "called *to be* saints" (Rom. 1:7; 1 Cor. 1:2). The words "to be," you will notice, are printed in italics, thereby indicating that those words are not in the original language but were added by the translators to make, what they thought would be, a clearer understanding of the passages. An accurate reading of these two verses is simply "called saints." Yet just as soon as we are "called saints" we are "called to be saints," or called to walk "as becometh saints." There is something not right about a human being behaving like an animal, or a full-grown man behaving like a small child. Nor is it right for a saint to be unsaintly.

Christian brethren, our God is a thrice-*holy* God (Isa. 6:3; Rev. 4:8); our Saviour is *holy* (Acts 4:27, 30); the Spirit who indwells us is the *Holy* Ghost (Acts 1:8); the Bible we read is the "*holy* scriptures" (Rom. 1:2); the name by which we are designated is "*holy* brethren" (1 Thess. 5:27; Heb. 3:1); ours is a "*holy* priesthood"

(1 Peter 2:5); the calling wherewith we are called is a *"holy* calling" (2 Tim. 1:9); when our Lord comes again He presents us *"holy* and unblameable and unreproveable in His sight" (Col. 1:22); and John points out the *"holy* city" (Rev. 21:2). Now that the end of the age is nearer than when we believed, Peter asks: "Seeing then that all these things shall be dissolved, what manner of persons ought ye to be in all holy conversation and godliness, looking for and hasting unto the coming of the day of God, wherein the heavens being on fire shall be dissolved, and the elements shall melt with fervent heat?" (2 Peter 3:11-12)

Included with the saints are "the *bishops* and *deacons";* the bishops or overseers being, as the word implies, the oversight brethren, and the deacons those who served in such capacities that would free pastors and teachers to give themselves to prayer and the ministry of the Word. We need such in our assemblies who will watch for souls and take up the oversight responsibilities. There is no record of these servants being elected or ordained by other men nor of their insisting upon obedience to their rules and regulations. Stephen and Philip are examples of early church deacons who, along with caring for the sick and the poor, ministered in the Word.

I find no warrant in the New Testament for the assumption that there is a distinction in clerical order and in ecclesiastical superiority for those who are called "bishops." Paul and Barnabas "ordained elders in every church" (Acts 14:23). I understand the words "elder" and "bishops" to be used interchangeably in the New Testament, the words carrying the same connotation. When Paul called together the elders of the church in

Ephesus, he enjoined upon them to "Take heed therefore
unto yourselves, and to all the flock, over the which the
Holy Ghost hath made you overseers, to feed the church
of God, which He hath purchased with His own blood"
(Acts 20:28).

Peter also writes: "The elders which are among you I
exhort, who am also an elder, and a witness of the sufferings of Christ, and also a partaker of the glory that
shall be revealed: Feed the flock of God which is among
you, taking the oversight thereof, not by constraint, but
willingly; not for filthy lucre, but of a ready mind" (1
Peter 5:1-2).

The local church must recognize both its spiritual and
social obligations, and this is the place where the offices
of bishop and deacon enter into the local scene. These
men were not the overseers of the pastors of numerous
local assemblies, but rather they were confined to work
among those in the individual congregation. Thus the
bishops (elders) were overseers of the spiritual needs in
the local congregation and the deacons looked after the
social, or material, needs. May God raise up men in our
churches to meet the needs of the people.

C. *The Salutation*

Grace be unto you, and *peace,* from God our Father, and
from the Lord Jesus Christ (Phil. 1:2).

Here are two rich spiritual commodities that Paul in-
vokes upon his readers. It is the apostle's desire for the
spiritual welfare of the saints, for saintliness in their lives.
He would have them know more and more of that divine
grace that makes the saints gracious.

Grace was the common Greek salutation and *peace* the

common Hebrew form of greeting. It was used in Bible times in the same manner as our "good morning." Paul combines the two in one, showing thereby that there is no difference between Jew and Gentile in Christ Jesus. The Occidental and Oriental greetings combine to suggest to us the oneness that exists between all true believers in our Lord Jesus Christ regardless of nationality.

Kenneth H. Wuest says that in its use among the Greeks, the word "grace" referred to a favor done by one Greek to another out of pure generosity of his heart and with no thought of reward; but New Testament usage of the word refers to that favor which God granted at Calvary when He, in the person of the Son of God, stepped down from His throne of sovereign judgment to take upon Himself the guilt and penalty of human sin. In the case of the Greek the favor was performed to a friend, never an enemy. In God's case the favor was done for a bitter enemy that hated Him. Now the moment a believing sinner is saved by God's grace, he becomes the recipient of that grace, and his life outwardly should show henceforth the same grace toward others. This is the fruit of the favor; therefore Paul senses the need for a continuous intake if there is to be the continuous outflow. I can be gracious so long as my supply of grace lasts.

In a later Epistle we are taught how and where we can receive the necessary supply of grace: "Let us therefore come boldly unto the throne of grace, that we may obtain mercy, and find grace to help in time of need" (Heb. 4:16). Grace is supplied to the believer as he comes to God in prayer. Concerning the apostles we read: "And when they had prayed . . . great grace was upon them all" (Acts 4:31, 33).

No Christian need be destitute of his needed portion of grace, for since we were justified through faith in Christ's blood, "We have access by faith into this grace" (Rom. 5:2).

We need an abundant supply of grace. We need it in our conversation in every word we utter, hence the exhortation: "Let your speech be alway with grace, seasoned with salt, that ye may know how to answer every man" (Col. 4:6). We need grace to carry us along in Christian service, so the injunction: "Let us have grace, whereby we may serve God acceptably with reverence and godly fear" (Heb. 12:28). With the multiplicity of "divers and strange doctrines . . . it is a good thing that the heart be established with grace" (Heb. 13:9).

The Christian who has not a sufficient supply of grace will show weakness in his spiritual reflexes; he will give forth with wrong words in a wrong spirit and be a blessing to no one; he will find himself failing in one undertaking and another; he will be unsuccessful in getting along with others. And how utterly tragic are these conditions among God's children when all the while we are "heirs together of the grace of life" (1 Peter 3:7), and have as our Heavenly Father "the God of all grace" (1 Peter 5:10), who "is able to make all grace abound toward you; that ye, always having all sufficiency in all things, may abound to every good work" (2 Cor. 9:8)!

The Bible says: "Grow in grace . . ." (2 Peter 3:18), and if we are not growing in grace, which is growth in the knowledge of our Lord Jesus Christ, it is because we are bypassing the path that leads to the inexhaustible storehouse of the superabundance of God's grace: namely, "the throne of grace." Oh, beloved, let us come, and let us come early enough at the start of each new day lest we fail of the grace of God in conduct and conversation. How wonderfully rich and blessed is the apostle's salutation, "Grace be unto you"!

But the salutation is not cut short with its expression of desire for grace. It continues, ". . . and *peace,* from God our Father, and from the Lord Jesus Christ."

We note the order of the words *grace* and *peace.* This order is theologically and experientially correct and it can never be reversed. There can be no peace, objectively or subjectively, where the sinner has not been saved by divine grace. First, grace; then, peace. And where the former is lacking, the latter will likewise be lacking. Some local congregations have little peace among their members simply because they are short on grace. Peace is lacking in some Christian homes for no other reason than that grace is lacking in the Christians' hearts. When a sinner gets saved by grace and continues to obtain grace for holy living, he is living peaceably with his brethren.

The peace in the salutation that Paul desires for God's children is not "peace with God." The armistice between the unbeliever and God is declared at the very moment of regeneration; for our Lord Jesus Christ, "having made peace through the blood of His cross" (Col. 1:20), effected the reconciliation. Every Christian is at peace with God since there is no condemnation before God. "Therefore being justified by faith, we have peace with God through our Lord Jesus Christ" (Rom. 5:1). When the soul is brought into harmony with the purposes of God, that soul commences a life of tranquility on a new plane.

The word "peace" means "to bind together," and this is exactly what the blood of Christ does for the believer: it binds him to God.

But I feel certain that Paul is not here expressing for the saints that which is already their portion and possession. Just as the Christian is constantly in need of grace to live triumphantly from day to day, so he is in need of peace to garrison his heart in the face of life's trials and troubles. Paul will have more to say about the "peace of God" a little later on in this Epistle. Suffice it to add here that grace and peace must come "from God our Father, and from the Lord Jesus Christ."

III. PRAISE

I thank my God upon every remembrance of you,
Always in every prayer of mine for you all making request
with joy.
For your fellowship in the gospel from the first day until
now;
Being confident of this very thing, that He which hath
begun a good work in you will perform it until the day of
Jesus Christ:
Even as it is meet for me to think this of you all, because
I have you in my heart; inasmuch as both in my bonds, and
in the defence and confirmation of the gospel, ye all are
partakers of my grace.
For God is my record, how greatly I long after you all
in the bowels of Jesus Christ.

Philippians 1:3-8

The body of the letter is introduced at verse three,
and it commences on a note of praise. My own heart is
blessed, as I write, by the mere thought of this strange
combination of persecution and praise. Paul the prisoner,
in bonds for the defense and confirmation of the gospel,
begins the body of his Epistle with rejoicing in his soul.
Nowhere in the religious writings of the world, outside
of the Bible, does one find evidence of inner peace and
praise under such provocation. The reason is obvious.
No religion outside of Christianity can produce a transformation of one's life equal to that of the Holy Spirit
in regeneration. None but a child of God, in the will of

God, can count it all joy when he comes by the varied trials of a troublesome life (James 1:2).

While Paul's rejoicing was the expression of an inward work of God, there is in Christianity a common bond among believers unequaled in the secret societies and sororities of this world. The Bible calls this sacred tie a "fellowship." The word is *koinonia* and it simply means "communion." The idea is that of a partnership, a sharing in common. Paul and the saints were partakers of, and partners in, a common gospel, and together they made up this holy fellowship. Wherever the gospel is preached and believed, a new community (or fellowship) of believers is created. This new fellowship is wholly foreign to the unregenerated, for the secret of it is within the hearts of those who have been born again. The word *koinonia* was used of the marriage bond, and it suggested a powerful common interest that could hold two or more persons together. In this instance it is that inevitable and obvious effect which is produced wherever Christ's saving gospel is received.

Paul uses the word at least five times in this Epistle (1:5; 2:1; 3:10; 4:14, 15), and it has been suggested by some commentators that this word "fellowship" is a key to a better understanding of the Book. Paul said: "I thank my God upon every remembrance of you . . . for your fellowship in the gospel" (Philippians 1:3, 5).

A. *Praise for a Controlled Fellowship*

This "fellowship" is "in the gospel." It is not controlled by a certain sect, nor a given social strata, nor a specified age bracket, nor a stated financial standing; it is *in the gospel*. The Christian community is not designated by

the insignia worn on a ring or a pin representing some
lodge or secret society, nor by a particular kind of hand-
shake, nor by a whispered password known only to those
initiated into this or that order. Christian fellowship is
a *"fellowship* of the Spirit" (Phil. 2:1). It has its commencement in the heart when we are born of the Spirit
(John 3:5; Titus 3:5), and it is controlled by the same
Holy Spirit.

All Christians are baptized by one Spirit into one body
(1 Cor. 12:13), and "the body is one" (1 Cor. 12:12).
When the Holy Spirit is in control of the body, the fellowship among the members of the body is unequaled on
earth, for then there is "love, joy, peace, longsuffering,
gentleness, goodness, faith, meekness, temperance" (Galatians 5:22-23). This is the "fruit of the Spirit" that
makes so wonderful "the fellowship of the Spirit." It is
not a forced, regimented fellowship, but a divinely-con-
trolled fellowship. Paul could write: " I thank my God
upon every remembrance of *you* (Phil. 1:3). Not because
of your possessions of this world's goods, not because
of your position in this world, not because of your power
in this world-system, but just because of "you." How
precious! What you are in Christ, God made you; what
you are, you are by His grace, and I thank Him for
"you." Praise God for this Spirit-controlled fellowship.

B. *Praise for a Continuing Fellowship*

Always in every prayer of mine for you all making request
with joy, for your *fellowship* in the gospel *from the first
day until now.*

Phil. 1:4-5

Approximately ten years had passed since that fellowship began, and "from the first day until now" it had continued. Now what was the secret of this continuing fellowship? *Thanksgiving* (vs. 3) and *prayer* (vs. 4). Not the one without the other, but both together. It is an indication of a Spirit-controlled heart when we praise and pray for the saints. This is exactly the way it should be.

The dispensation of the Holy Spirit began with this continuing spirit in the lives of the new converts, for we read: "And they continued stedfastly in . . . *fellowship* . . . and in prayers" (Acts 2:42).

There was no conflict, no confusion, but continuance. A continuing fellowship is a prayer fellowship. Today a very narrow conception of fellowship prevails. If we attend the same church, recite the same creed, say the same prayers, eat at the same church supper, and socialize with the same crowd, we call this Christian fellowship. But is it? For years I have watched all of these things going on among professing Christians where there was often little conception of true fellowship in the gospel. Among Christians there may be difficulties and disappointments along the way, but never a disruption where there is prayer fellowship. True Christian fellowship is a continuing experience, "from the first day until now." Praise God for a continuing fellowship.

C. *Praise for a Confirmed Fellowship*

Being confident of this very thing, that He which hath begun a good work in you will perform it until the day of Jesus Christ.

Phil. 1:6

The word "confident" here means persuaded. This fellowship could not fall apart. It was established. Local

assemblies may fall apart, church organizations may
crumble, professing Christians may engage in fighting
instead of fellowshiping, but all of this division and destruction is the result of a false foundation. Being confident
of this very thing, that *He* is able—and will—complete
what *He* has begun.

Who founded your local assembly? Who organized your
church? Who started your little Bible study group? Who
instigated your regular gatherings for "fellowship"? Paul's
confidence was in that which God was going to do.
Gamaliel spoke a great truth when he said: "If this
counsel or this work be of men, it will come to nought:
But if it be of God, ye cannot overthrow it; lest haply
ye be found even to fight against God" (Acts 5:38, 39).

No local assembly can enjoy a continuing fellowship
if He did not begin His good work in its members. Strife
and seclusion, faction and falling apart, speak only that
something was begun by someone in whose heart Jesus
Christ had never begun His good work. Paul was confident
that nothing could come between them since his confidence
was based on a sure Foundation: namely, Christ Himself. Those He saves He always sustains.

Then, too, the "good work," the divine work of regeneration, was always manifest in the Philippian saints.
Paul could not recall anything in their actions or attitude
that did not give evidence of the new birth. "I thank
my God upon every remembrance of you" (Phil. 1:3).
Every time his mind reminisced about them, Paul vividly
pictured their "good works" which were but the fruits
of the Spirit's "good work." There was the true spirit of
Christian love shown by Lydia (Acts 16:15) and the
jailer (Acts 16:33-34), those first converts in Philippi

and those who doubtless took hold of those who were saved later. How rare in our age is such a fellowship! How sweet to Paul was such a memory! His confidence was well grounded since it was not in the saints, but rather in the Author and Finisher of their faith. What a ground for confidence! Praise God for a confirmed fellowship.

D. *Praise for a Compassionate Fellowship*

. . . I have you in my heart . . . for God is my record, how greatly I long after you all in the bowels of Jesus Christ.
Phil. 1:7-8

Paul's praise soars higher and higher in this paragraph as it reaches a new peak in this personal touch. The word "meet" in verse seven means "right." He adds that it is right for him to think this way about them because he carries them in his heart. Many of the earliest converts he had been a means of winning to Christ. It was only right, and still is, that Christians should carry on their hearts their spiritual children in the faith. The saints at Philippi were not a nuisance on Paul's nerves, not a weight upon his mind, but a joy in his heart. Though himself in prison, he was rejoicing in their "fellowship in the gospel." In their place, and in their way, they were sharing in the defense and confirmation of the gospel. The idea in the word "fellowship" is that of joint participation. In this instance it was participation in the divine project of spreading the good news of the gospel.

True Christian fellowship is the source of sweetest memories, and such memories can serve a blessed purpose in times of affliction. What kind of memories have we left with our friends? Do they give thanks upon every remembrance of us? In their affliction can they derive comfort as they think of us? No doubt with most of us the record could be greatly improved. There is no bond that can comfort in fair weather and in foul like the blood of Calvary's cross. It is in times of affliction that the acid test is made. The Philippians had proved themselves, for Paul wrote: "Notwithstanding ye have well done, that ye did communicate [fellowship] with my affliction" (Phil. 4:14).

These Philippians had become joint partners in Paul's troubles; they were sharers in his affliction. A right relation with God will result in a new relation with others. This new relation is a compassionate fellowship produced by the mutual experience of receiving the tender mercies and compassion of Jesus Christ. It is Calvary that binds our hearts in Christian love. Paul calls God to witness of this: "For God is my record [or witness], how greatly I long after you all in the bowels of Jesus Christ" (Phil. 1:8).

The word "bowels" (see also Phil. 2:1) is always in the plural, and apart from its one reference to the physical organs of the intestines in Acts 1:18, it means *affection, tender mercies, compassion.* To the ancients the bowels were regarded as the seat of the emotions. As Jesus Christ yearned after them, and him, so Paul would follow the divine pattern.

In Christ, and for Christ's sake, we must know something of such compassion. When we love and long after the souls of men with the passion of Christ, our lives and local assemblies will be outlets for the sweeping, saving fires of divine love. Our calling as Christians is to a life that exemplifies, in letters large and plain, the affection and compassion of our Lord Jesus Christ.

With just such affection and compassion, Paul and the saints at Philippi were bound inseparably in sweet fellowship. Little wonder his heart was filled with praise! And so would be yours and mine if we only knew such a compassionate, confirmed, continuing, and Spirit-controlled fellowship in the gospel. May our heavenly Father grant that for us it may be so!

IV. PRABYER

And this I pray, that your love may abound yet more and
more in knowledge and in all judgment;

That ye may approve things that are excellent; that ye
may be sincere and without offence till the day of Christ;

Being filled with the fruits of righteousness, which are
by Jesus Christ, unto the glory and praise of God.

Philippians 1:9-11

"And this I pray." Now these are not mere empty
words with Paul as is so often the case with some of us.
We talk to others about prayer, but fail to talk to God
in prayer about others. We tell our friends we are going
to pray for them but we do not remain true to our word.
The great apostle was a man of prayer. The prayers of
Paul, especially his prison prayers, are rich in content
and character. It is not difficult to imagine that every
movement of his pen was accompanied by prayer, and
that his petitions were made up of the very desires
expressed in these verses.

The genuine and pure longings of a sincere and compassionate heart quite naturally take the form of prayer.
The reason is obvious. There is only One who is able to
satisfy the longing soul. "The Lord . . . satisfieth the longing soul, and filleth the hungry soul with goodness"
(Psalm 107:8, 9).

If we can be certain that God will give us the desires
of our hearts when we delight ourselves in Him and His

things, and we can be certain that He will (Psalm 37:4), then we are foolish indeed when we fail to pray.

The apostle had a threefold burden upon his heart for the saints at Philippi, and it is for these he prays.

A. *Prayer for a Fuller Expression of Love*

And this I pray, that your love may abound yet more and more in knowledge and in all judgment.

Now love was not lacking in the local assembly in Philippi, as his praise of them was revealed; but he desires for them that the love they already had manifested may now abound. He is praying for fuller and more fervent expression of love.

Love is the first and foremost of all Christian characteristics (Galatians 5:22), and the greatest of them all (1 Cor. 13:13). Love is the foremost of all the commandments of our Lord (John 13:34), and the most convincing testimony to the unsaved (John 13:35). Love is a force that is most compelling (2 Cor. 5:14) and it will continue when other gifts have ceased (1 Cor. 13:8). Its exercise is indispensable to successful Christian living, so that Paul prays for an overflow of love in the lives of the saints.

The word "abound" is the verb form of the noun *abundance*. To have an abundance of something is to have an exceeding measure, above the ordinary. Paul prays that the believers will be provided richly with an abundance of love, that the measure of their love will continue to increase. See how closely abounding love is associated with prayer, the reason being that God alone can give the supply. In a later Epistle, Paul wrote: "And the Lord make you to increase and abound in love one toward another, and toward all men, even as we do toward you" (1 Thess. 3:12).

"This is my prayer then," says Paul, "that the Lord may enlarge your capacity for more than an ordinary measure of love." He desired from them a more fervent expression of that divine love that can be known only from the action it prompts.

Most of us have doubtless felt a terrible dearth of love in our own hearts. How often have some of us, in our spiritual poverty, longed to abound in this rich treasure! Our attitudes and actions are at times so demonstrative of our deficiency that we are driven to deplore ourselves and to wish that we could display more of the love of Christ. Well, dear ones in Christ, we can. If your heart longs to abound in love, as does mine, let us together pursue the pages of God's Word as we search both our hearts and the truth of God.

In his prayer for abounding love, Paul gives to us a key as to its source. He says: "That your love may abound yet more and more in *knowledge*." Christian love is never a matter of mere sentimentality, no mere stirring of the emotions brought on by circumstances. Christian love is controlled by the Holy Spirit through the truth, that is, through the Word of God. Thus its fullest and most fervent exercise can spring only from a *knowledge* of the truth. The heart that is not guided by God's Word cannot unselfishly love God nor man. The life distinguished by Christian love has developed in Christian knowledge, since growth is a law of spiritual life as it is of natural life. The newborn babe comes into its infancy, and then passes to childhood, to youth, to manhood. Believing sinners are said by our Lord to be "born again" (John 3:3). Then they pass through the stages of "little children," "young men," and "fathers" (1 John 2:12-14).

The essential food for this developing process is the Word of God. Peter left us these tremendous passages that explain this: "As newborn babes, desire the sincere milk of the word, that ye may grow thereby" (1 Peter 2:2). "And beside this, giving all diligence, add to your faith virtue; and to virtue *knowledge*" (2 Peter 1:5). "But grow in grace, and in the knowledge of our Lord and Saviour Jesus Christ" (2 Peter 3:18). These verses teach us that Christian growth is dependent first upon a knowledge of the Word of God. Now let us apply this principle to Paul's prayer "that your *love* may abound yet more and more in *knowledge*."

Let me say at this point that provision has been made for every child of God to abound in love. When we were born again we received a new nature, the very nature of God. Peter said that we are "partakers of the divine nature" (2 Peter 1:4). Love is one of the essential moral attributes of God. One of the first truths we learn in story as children in Sunday school is that "God is love" (1 John 4:8, 16). Therefore, when God takes up His residence in the believer's heart, the seed of divine love is planted at once by the Holy Spirit, "because the love of God is shed abroad in our hearts by the Holy Ghost which is given unto us" (Rom. 5:5). Let no Christian entertain the false idea that he has been given a lesser portion of love than another. If the love is not there, the Lord is not there. His love has not been distributed in drops by measure, more to some and less to others; but rather has it been "shed abroad," that is, profusely diffused, in all its fullness upon all who are born of the Spirit.

Why, then, are some of us short in the display of divine love? Why has it developed in some and lain dormant in others? If I understand correctly the meaning of Paul's prayer, then we have an answer, in part at least, to our first question. Where there is no exercise of love there is either *no life* or *no learning*. The Apostle John shows us the possibility of *no life:* "We know that we have passed from death unto life, because we love the brethren. He that loveth not his brother abideth in death. Whosoever hateth his brother is a murderer: and ye know that no murderer hath eternal life abiding in him" (1 John 3:14, 15). No language could be plainer. God is life and God is love, and you cannot have the one without the other.

But in the case of a Christian failing to show forth the fruit of love, he is guilty of inexcusable ignorance of the Word of God or insubordination to the Word of God. Since right knowledge is an aid to a fuller expression of love, let us pursue a bit of it.

One of the first lessons to be learned is that the debt of love is never fully paid: "Owe no man any thing, but to love one another: for he that loveth another hath fulfilled the law" (Rom. 13:8).

It is possible to acquit ourselves of all obligations except love. We may pay the obligation of obedience to higher powers and those placed upon us through tribute or taxes, but the debt of love will always remain unpaid.

We have never fully learned our obligations, therefore we can never fully live them. Ignorance is inexcusable if our taxes and revenues to our government are unpaid. It is more so with respect to love, so we must carry on to learn.

Paul suggests a way in which we abound in love. "For, brethren, ye have been called unto liberty; only use not liberty for an occasion to the flesh, but by love serve one another. For all the law is fulfilled in one word, even in this; Thou shalt love thy neighbour as thyself" (Gal. 5:13-14).

Here we are taught how we may reduce the debt of love. It is by serving one another, for in so doing we fulfill the Law of God. In the Golden Rule (so called), our Lord showed us this very fact. "Therefore all things whatsoever ye would that men should do to you, do ye even so to them: for this is the law and the prophets" (Matt. 7:12). Love's law is to put myself in another's place, and then act toward him as though he were myself, for all the law is summed up in the one word "love" (Lev. 19:18). "Jesus said unto him, Thou shalt love the Lord thy God with all thy heart, and with all thy soul, and with all thy mind. This is the first and great commandment. And the second is like unto it, Thou shalt love thy neighbour as thyself. On these two commandments hang all the law and the prophets" (Matt. 22:37-40). This great truth was reiterated by the apostles (Rom. 13:8-9; Galatians 5:13-14; Ephesians 5:25-30; James 2:8). The man who loves God as a Christian will not break His commandments. If we love one another we will not do wrong nor think wrongly of each other, but rather will we go out of our way to serve one another. Love is the motive of true service, and such service is without constraint. Because Christ loved His disciples He stooped in lowly service to wash their feet (John 13:1-5). Because He loved the Church He gave Himself for it (Eph. 5:25). This is the love planted in the heart of the believer by the Holy Spirit, whose chief essence is self-sacrifice for the benefit of others.

Among men the natural inclination is to be served. Or if we sense a need for service and we have more than enough money for ourselves, we sometimes attempt to discharge our obligation of love by paying someone else to discharge it for us. I feel certain that the giving of money with such a motive, no matter how large the amount, is no labor of love and is not acceptable to God. We are servants all. Jesus said: "Whosoever will be great among you, shall be your minister: and whosoever of you will be the chiefest, shall be servant of all" (Mark 10:43-44). When we are slow to serve we are short on love.

"And this I pray, that your *love* may abound yet more and more in *knowledge*." You see, knowledge safeguards love. Have we learned a lesson here? Have we gained this knowledge that true love serves others? If so, then let us go forward to pay off a bit more of our obligation. Don't forget, rate others as high as you rate yourself! The world says that "love is blind," but really it is not. Love is alert and ever looking for an opportunity to serve others. Blind love is not divine love. True love sharpens our perception to see opportunites for service.

Oh, beloved, do we not want our love to grow? Do we

not want it to abound yet more and more? The demands upon our love are so great it must experience a continuous growth. For this I pray.

B. *Prayer for a Finer Evaluation of Life*

That ye may approve things that are excellent; that ye may be sincere and without offence till the day of Christ.
Phil. 1:10

Paul's knowledge of human nature was profound. He knew how weak most of us are in evaluating correctly the things of this life. Some of us are a long time learning how to estimate wisely so as to choose the things that are worthful. We are short on those discerning and discriminating powers. Discernment, like love, needs to be developed in us We do not permit our children to make their own decisions in life until we have seen some evidence of the development of those powers. But even in adults, there is sometimes the display of childishness, that undeveloped and immature characteristic of the infantile.

How sad, and often how tragic, is this weakness among professing Christians! I am not thinking of new converts, but of men and women who have for many years named the name of our Lord Jesus Christ and still continue in an undeveloped state in this matter of discernment.

The apostle prays that the saints may "approve" the things that are excellent. In order to approve the thing that is excellent, we must be able to distinguish between what is good and what is best. It is not as though Paul were praying for them that they might be able to discern between good and bad, for it requires no unusual keenness to discriminate between right and wrong; but rather that they should know how to choose the highest, the things that transcend. Making right choices is one of life's greatest assets, and for this Paul prays.

Now in order to approve things that are excellent there must be a standard with which we can harmonize our choice. That standard is not to be found in the varied philosophies of man. If we made choices to please our friends and acquaintances, there could be no set standard simply because the ideas of men as to what is best are many and mixed. The highest possible standard is arrived at only as we are guided in our decisions by what would best please and honor God. As we develop in this gift of discernment there is a growing appreciation of those things that are best in God's eyes as set forth in His Word, and that becomes the finest quality of Christian character. The more the Christian exercises the gift of discernment and thereby decides for the best in God's eyes, the more will he develop a taste for the highest. The apostle's prayer indicates a need for proper ballast and balance in determining the excellence or defects in a person or thing.

Most commentators suggest that the phrase "approve things that are excellent" means *to test things that differ*. The meanings are almost necessary to each other in this passage, for we cannot approve what is excellent apart from testing the things that differ. Again, as a knowledge of God's Word is essential to a fuller expression of love, that same Word is the test for a finer evaluation of life. Actually the Word of God is the discerner, the judge in making a final decision, since our discernment and decisions are to be based on that Word. In ourselves we are not skilled to judge, but the Word of God is. "For the word of God is quick, and powerful, and sharper than any two-edged sword, piercing even to the dividing asunder of soul and spirit, and of the joints and marrow, and is a discerner of the thoughts and intents of the heart" (Heb. 4:12).

The word "discerner" is a noun naming the living and active Word of God. We do not know fully our own thoughts with all the designs and purposes of the heart; hence it is unsafe to decide without proper guidance. We need Someone who knows us better than we know ourselves, and that One is God who created us. The Christian can discriminate and pen judgment only as he knows what is best. The best is in the Bible. God's Word is the safest discerner.

The Greek word for "discerner" is *kritikos,* from which we get our English word "critic." The Bible is the best critic, or judge of life's highest values because it discerns the thoughts and intents of the heart. You see, what a man thinks and plans in his heart, that is what he will be in real life. "For as he thinketh in his heart, so is he" (Prov. 23:7). If we would approve the excellent at all times, we must submit to have our secret thoughts and purposes examined by the light of God's Word.

Some Christians approach a dissipation level expending time and energy on things that have no real worth. Whether we are reading a book or magazine, listening to music, indulging in some pleasure or pastime, or even sitting through an evening with friends, we should exercise great care in discriminating so that we "approach the things that are excellent."

The prayer continues with the words, "that ye may be *sincere.*" The word "sincere" comes from two Latin words, *sine* (meaning *without*), and *cera* (meaning *wax*), without wax. For a number of years the writer was a retail furniture salesman. Before a piece of furniture was delivered to the customer, it was checked carefully for scratches and other types of blemishes. Any crack or scratch would be filled in with a wax of matching color. Technically speaking, a piece of furniture with a crack that had been filled in with wax was not in reality as in appearance. Ancient dealers in porcelain performed the same operation on pieces of porcelain ware that had cracked while being fired. An honest dealer would describe a perfect piece with the words *sine cera* (without wax). If the customer should doubt the dealer's honesty, he needed only to hold it to the light, and if the object in question had been repaired with wax, the filled-in crack would at once be manifest.

Paul's prayer is for sincerity among Christians. As we expose ourselves to the light of God's Word, we should be found without wax, being actually as we appear. We are to be men of transparent character, our hearts being on the inside what we appear to be without.

The Christian is the opposite of the hypocrite. This is convincingly illustrated by Paul as it relates to Christian love. The apostle writes: "Let love be without dissimulation" (Rom. 12:9). He is saying that our love is to be without hypocrisy, without pretence. In other words, we should not be two-faced, but rather "prove the sincerity of your love" (2 Cor. 8:8).

Further on in our chapter the apostle speaks of those who "preach Christ . . . not sincerely" (Phil. 1:16). Here he refers to those who occupy the office of Christ's ministers but whose motives are not pure. What a challenge to every one of us who hold this high and holy office! Our churches need more preaching and more preachers "without wax." God's standards for a Christian pulpit do not allow for any preacher to preach what he does not practice. No preacher has any right to expect his hearers to adhere to one code of ethics while he himself lives by some lesser code. The Holy Scriptures, wherever obeyed, will produce a sincere and holy life. Peter wrote: "As newborn babes, desire the *sincere* milk of the word, that ye may grow thereby" (1 Pet. 2:2).

The Word of God is "sincere," that is, *guileless*. Notice how this exhortation from Peter is preceded directly by another which says: "Wherefore laying aside all malice, and all guile" (1 Pet. 2:1). The words *sincere* and *guile* (or guileless) are translations of the one word *adolos*. A sincere (or guileless) life is the fruit of obedience to the sincere (or guileless) Word of God. Beloved, we need not be two-faced. We can, and should be, sincere, without wax, without guile. Our Lord Jesus Christ met such a man, and of Nathanael He testified: "Behold an Israelite indeed, in whom is no guile!" (John 1:47). Does He testify this of you and me? Be sincere!

A reason is now given why Christians should be sincere: namely, that we might be *"without offence."* The life of God's child must be so ordered that he gives no one an occasion to stumble or fall. W. E. Vine says that the noun *skandalon* (translated offence) originally was the name of that part of a trap to which the bait is attached, hence the snare which causes one to fall into the trap. As a Christian I am to give no occasion for anyone to fall into Satan's trap. Paul warns against any abuse of Christian liberty that might offend or cause to stumble. Read carefully the inspired discourse in First Corinthians 8. It concludes with Paul's personal response to what the Spirit says: "But when ye sin so against the brethren, and wound their weak conscience, ye sin against Christ. Wherefore, if meat make my brother to offend, I will eat no flesh while the world standeth, lest I make my brother to offend" (1 Cor. 8:12-13).

Roy L. Laurin writes of a lovely tribute a sister paid to her dead brother. As she stood beside his body weeping, she placed his hand in hers, and with strokes of affection she said: "This hand never struck me. It was a hand without offence." When love is abounding and sincerity is the condition of the heart, God will give to us hands and feet and eyes and lips "without offence."

"Let us not therefore judge one another any more: but judge this rather, that no man put a stumblingblock or an occasion to fall in his brother's way" (Romans 14:13). The believer, like his Bible, is to be wholly devoid of any false mixture. He is to be sincere, guileless, without offence "till the day of Christ." When our blessed Lord returns, will He find us utterly sincere, through and through?

Paul engaged in a spiritually healthful exercise that is good for us all. "And herein do I exercise myself, to have always a conscience void of offence toward God, and toward men" (Acts 24:16). "Give none offence, neither to the Jews, nor to the Gentiles, nor to the Church of God" (1 Cor. 10:32).

C. *Prayer for a Fuller Experience of Righteousness*

Being filled with the fruits of righteousness which are by Jesus Christ, unto the glory and praise of God.

Phil. 1:11

Right living is the fruit of right learning; proper deportment of proper doctrine; correct behavior of correct belief. A concern of every Christian should be that his life present that fruit of Christianity commensurate with his profession of its facts. It is this very thing for which Paul prays. A blighted orchard bearing no fruit is a sorry sight. Sadder still is the fruitless life of a child of God!

The word "fruit" has been defined as that which is produced by the inherent energy of a living organism. An oak tree is the only possible fruit that can be produced by the inherent energy within the acorn. Like begets like. As is stated numerous times in Genesis 1, each seed reproduces "after its kind."

The word "fruit" is used of the human body. In His humanity Christ is said to be the "fruit" of Abraham's loins, that is, He was to be born of one who would be a direct descendant of David (Acts 2:30). When speaking of our Lord, Elisabeth said to Mary: "Blessed is the fruit of thy womb" (Luke 1:42).

Metaphorically, the word "fruit" is used of the Christian's attitude and actions, that outward expression of an unseen Power working within, the character of the fruit being a clear indication of the character of the power producing it. We can know a tree by its fruit. Our Lord said: "Beware of false prophets, which come to you in sheep's clothing, but inwardly they are ravening wolves. Ye shall know them by their fruits. Do men gather grapes of thorns, or figs of thistles?

"Even so every good tree bringeth forth good fruit; but a corrupt tree bringeth forth evil fruit. A good tree cannot bring forth evil fruit, neither can a corrupt tree bring forth good fruit. Every tree that bringeth not forth good fruit is hewn down, and cast into the fire. Wherefore by their fruits ye shall know them" (Matt. 7:15-20).

The fruit of righteousness, for which Paul prays, can not be produced in an unregenerate heart. Before the fruit can be produced the seed must be planted. The Bible never appeals to a man to express the fruit of regeneration if he has not experienced the fact of regeneration. One must possess life in order to live. Therefore, the apostle's prayer for the fruit of righteousness is for believers only, since the righteousness of God is one thing of which every unbeliever is destitute.

The character or quality of being right or just has an objective standard to be found nowhere in the writings of men. Human standards of right and wrong vary widely, and at their best they fall far short of God's standards. Human righteousness and divine righteousness differ in kind. The Bible says: "But we are all as an unclean thing, and all our righteousnesses are as filthy rags" (Isaiah 64:6).

Righteousness in Scripture is sometimes set forth in the symbol of a garment. Human righteousness, when set alongside God's righteousness, is a dirty garment. You see, the best that a moral man, under law, can do is produce self-righteousness, and this, when held against the pure background of God's righteousness, is banned. At the marriage of the Lamb to His Bride, the wedding garment is described as "fine linen, clean and white: for the fine linen is the righteousness of saints" (Rev. 19:8).

There are two righteousnesses described in the Bible. One is the righteousness which is of the law, a self-right-eousness that is established by self-effort and that takes pride in its religious pedigree. The other is the righteousness of God which is reckoned to the believing sinner. This latter is of grace and comes by faith (Rom. 3:21, 22, 25, 26; 4:3-6). It is an imputed righteousness based upon our simple faith in the finished work of our Lord Jesus Christ (2 Cor. 5:21). This is a garment divinely provided that sinners might be made fit for God's presence. Its ground is the substitutionary death of the guiltless One. The imputed righteousness based upon a substitute is seen in type in the coats of skins provided by God for Adam and Eve (Genesis 3:21), in contrast to the fig leaves of self-righteousness which they made themselves (Gen. 3:7).

Now the desire in the heart of every believer should be like that expressed by Paul later in the Philippian Epistle: "That I may . . . be found in Him, not having mine own righteousness . . . but the righteousness which is of God by faith" (Phil. 3:9).

In Him we have a righteousness, that is, a right standing. When we meet Him, we want to be found in a right state. This was Paul's desire for himself and his prayer for us when he says: "Being filled with the fruits of righteousness, which are by Jesus Christ, unto the glory and praise of God" (Phil. 1:11).

The Christian is appointed to bear the fruit of righteousness. Jesus said: "Ye have not chosen Me, but I have chosen you, and ordained you, that ye should go and bring forth fruit, and that your fruit should remain: that whatsoever ye shall ask of the Father in My Name, He may give it you" (John 15:16). Our Lord is addressing Himself to the eleven disciples and to all whom they represented, telling them — and us — that He has ordained (appointed) us to fruit-bearing.

The word "fruit" occurs eight times in this chapter, and it is associated closely with our relation to Christ and His expectation of us. The branches on a vine are intended to bear fruit.

God intended that Israel should bear fruit for Him before the other nations, but Israel failed. The prophet Hosea wrote: "Israel is an empty vine, he bringeth forth fruit unto himself: according to the multitude of his fruit he hath increased the altars; according to the goodness of his land they have made goodly images" (Hosea 10:1).

It was Israel's divided heart (Hosea 10:2) that caused her to be selfish and fruitless and ultimately set aside by God. The prophet Isaiah likewise pictures the vine. "Now will I sing to my wellbeloved a song of my beloved touching his vineyard. My wellbeloved hath a vineyard in a very fruitful hill:

"And he fenced it, and gathered out the stones thereof, and planted it with the choicest vine, and built a tower in the midst of it, and also made a winepress therein: and he looked that it should bring forth grapes, and it brought forth wild grapes . . . . For the vineyard of the Lord of hosts is the house of Israel, and the men of Judah his pleasant plant: and he looked for judgment but behold oppression; for righteousness, but behold a cry" (Isaiah 5:1-2, 7).

And so God rejected Israel, the vine planted in the earth for the express purpose of bearing fruit unto Him but failing in that commission (Jer. 2:21). Instead she brought forth a natural and ungrafted fruit, "wild grapes," which means a fruit with a stench. Human nature, without Christ being grafted in, cannot produce the fruit of righteousness.

The Lord Jesus, knowing Israel's failure, says:

"I AM the true vine, and My Father is the husbandman. Every branch in Me that beareth not fruit He taketh away: and every branch that beareth fruit, He purgeth it, that it may bring forth more fruit.

"I am the vine, ye are the branches: He that abideth in Me, and I in him, the same bringeth forth much fruit: for without Me ye can do nothing" (John 15:1-2,5).

The glory of a vine is its fruit. How solemn a thought that the Lord is depending on us for a display of His glory! The fruit of righteousness is a godly life as seen in that ninefold cluster of the fruit of the Holy Spirit: "Love, joy, peace, longsuffering, gentleness, goodness, faith, meekness, temperance" [or self-control] (Galatians 5:22-23). The fruit of righteousness is that person whom, by our godly living and personal testimony, we influence to Jesus Christ (Rom. 1:13).

Paul's prayer is that these things might fill our lives, for they constitute the fruit of righteousness; and all are the result of our abiding in Christ and are unto the glory and praise of God. Our apple tree neither counts its own apples nor boasts in their quality: it merely produces them. "Herein is My Father glorified, that ye bear much fruit; so shall ye be My disciples" (John 15:8).

V. PLEASURE

But I would ye should understand, brethren, that the things which happened unto me have fallen out rather unto the furtherance of the gospel;

So that my bonds in Christ are manifest in all the palace, and in all other places;

And many of the brethren in the Lord, waxing confident by my bonds, are much more bold to speak the word without fear.

Some indeed preach Christ even of envy and strife; and some also of good will:

The one preach Christ of contention, not sincerely, supposing to add affliction to my bonds:

But the other of love, knowing that I am set for the defence of the gospel.

What then? notwithstanding, every way, whether in pretence, or in truth, Christ is preached; and I therein do rejoice, yea, and will rejoice.

Philippians 1:12-18

A real test of the genuineness of Christian profession is witnessed when one finds himself under pressure, provocation, or persecution. Without appearing to be critical of anyone, I venture to say that victory amidst the vicissitudes of this life is rare indeed. Our reaction to a sudden, unexpected change of condition or circumstances shows up a weakness in many of us. Some Christians are thrown completely off balance if anyone disagrees with them, and under more trying circumstances they go completely to pieces.

The Christian's attitude toward the restrictions of life

will determine largely the depth of spiritual experience. The advantage that life's limitations can have in my personal life is a matter which only I can decide. If I whine and wince under the circumstances, I am shriveling my own soul and showing a shallowness of Christian experience. If I can be content and remain consistent above the circumstances, I help myself and others.

The Apostle Paul was outstanding in maintaining serenity and steadfastness in the face of sorrow and suffering. He looked upon all his adversities as being divinely sent with a God-directed purpose. When discussing his thorn in the flesh, he testified: "Therefore I take pleasure in infirmities, in reproaches, in necessities, in persecutions, in distresses for Christ's sake: for when I am weak, then am I strong" (2 Cor. 12:10).

Here is a key to the problem of life's adversities. It is the attitude of my heart. It is not God's giving me what I desire, but rather it is my attitude in accepting what God sends. The words "take pleasure" mean "to think well." In thinking well of his infirmity, that is, by taking the right attitude toward his adversity, the effect was strength. To be strong in weakness is a paradox in Christian experience not known to the unbeliever and too little known among the saved. What is your attitude when you are suddenly stopped short of a goal that was a part of your planning? Do you resist the change? Do you resent the circumstance? The verses before us in the Philippian letter show how Paul's pleasure, his well-thinking, in tribulation effected triumph.

Now remember that Paul is writing from prison in Rome. For years Paul had carried in his heart a burden for the poor souls in Rome. In one letter which he sent "to all that be in Rome," he said: "So, as much as in me is, I am ready to preach the gospel to you that are at Rome also" (Rom. 1:15). "After these things were ended, Paul purposed in the spirit, when he had passed through Macedonia and Achaia, to go to Jerusalem, saying, After I have been there, I must also see Rome" (Acts 19:21). "And the night following the Lord stood by him, and said, Be of good cheer, Paul: for as thou hast testified of Me in Jerusalem, so must thou bear witness also at Rome" (Acts 23:11).

Little did he realize the conditions under which he would go to Rome. He had prayed that, if it be "by the will of God," he might have a "prosperous journey" (Rom. 1:10). Now we may not think that his request was granted, for God did not give him a prosperous journey as we might look upon prosperity. He did not go as a preacher, but as a prisoner. Of course, if we look at prosperity in terms of the material, then Paul did have a prosperous journey, for had he gone as a preacher he would have paid his own fare. As it was, the Roman government gave him free passage. At any rate, he is in Rome, and though he sits bound in a dungeon, God's servant is a happy, contented Christian. Whatever could he rejoice in with death waiting at the door? He was restrained from active preaching, and the enemies of the gospel were already at work tearing down his reputation. Still his heart was glad. Why?

A. *Pleasure in a Greater Distribution of the Gospel*

The gospel of Christ is a major subject of this Epistle and the dissemination of this blessed truth was Paul's whole life. He mentions the gospel no less than six times

in the first chapter (1:5, 7, 12, 17, 27). The gospel is the
Christian evangel, the good news that Christ died for our
sins, that He was buried, and that He rose again the third
day according to the Scriptures (1 Cor. 15:1-4). Any
distribution of the gospel gladdened his heart. Now he
takes pleasure in his persecution because it has resulted
in someone's hearing about Christ. Why sink in the slough
of despond with the opportunity at hand to preach Christ?
"The things which happened unto me have fallen out
rather unto the furtherance of the gospel" (Phil. 1:12).

To Paul, being detained in a dungeon only resulted in a
wider diffusion of the gospel. Handcuffed to a Roman
guard gave him an opportunity he might never have had
as a free man. It was soon spread throughout the palace
that this man was no ordinary prisoner. Change guards
and you merely give to Paul a new audience to tell the
good news of salvation.

It is possible that God will place us in a circumstance,
undesirable and even unwanted as far as we are concerned, but a place of His choosing, that we might win
someone to the Lord Jesus Christ. With Paul it was an
opportunity to witness to Caesar's household, to those
men forming the praetorian guard. And some were saved,
to be certain, for before this Epistle was completed, God's
servant was telling of "the saints . . . that are of Caesar's
household" (Phil. 4:22). If Paul had not been a prisoner
he could never have approached the highest dignitaries
and the lowest servants in the palace at Rome. "So that
my bonds in Christ are manifest in all the palace, and in
all other places" (Phil. 1:13).

Many a Christian, taking advantage of a God-directed

illness on a hospital bed has led a patient, a nurse, or a doctor to receive Jesus Christ. Do we rise above our circumstances to seize them as an opportunity to spread the gospel? Who can know the joy that must have filled the hearts of Paul and Silas when, as prisoners together in the jail at Philippi, they led the guard to Christ? And now again Paul finds great joy in giving his testimony for his Saviour. He could say that "the things which happened unto me" furthered the gospel rather than fettered it. And this is exactly what the Lord had predicted: "But before all these, they shall lay their hands on you, and persecute you, delivering you up to the synagogues, and into prisons, being brought before kings and rulers for My Name's sake. And it shall turn to you for a testimony" (Luke 21:12-13).

The things that appear to happen to you and me are all a part of God's plan and should contribute toward the progress of God's Word. I am glad the translators put into italics the words "*which happened.*" They were not in the original but have been added. The word "happen" conveys the idea of something coming to pass by chance without previous expectation or prevision. A thing is said to *happen* when no plan or design is manifest. But in God's providential dealings with His children there is never the element of chance. You see, Paul was bound, but the Word of God was not. It never is! "Wherein I suffer trouble, as an evil doer, even unto bonds; but the word of God is not bound" (2 Tim. 2:9).

The brave apostle was in bonds, but he was bound in order that he might broadcast the blessing of the gospel. *Trouble* cannot bind the gospel for it is the mighty comforter in time of trouble. *Time* cannot bind it, for it is both timely and timeless. Time may condemn some writings to impassivity and impotence, but it cannot and will not condemn the ageless Word of God. In this God's servant takes pleasure and praises Him regardless of the circumstances.

B. *Pleasure in a Greater Daring for the Gospel*

Secondly, Paul rejoiced: "And many of the brethren in the Lord, waxing confident by my bonds, are much more bold to speak the word without fear" (Phil. 1:14).

It was common information that Paul was in prison awaiting a trial before Nero. This knowledge of the apostle's persecution for the gospel's sake had telling effect upon the Christians in Rome. Many who were timid about testifying for Christ now were possessed of a new daring. Courage was replacing cowardice in many of them. A new bravery and boldness was beginning to take hold. Persecution was causing progress.

Elsewhere Luke gives to us a thrilling account of courage in chains. Peter and John were put in prison for preaching Christ. The next day they were brought to trial before the hierarchy, but the court trial was turned into a preaching service, the sermon concluding with one of the greatest gospel texts in the New Testament: namely, Acts 4:12. Then Luke describes the audience of legal advisors: "Now when they saw the boldness of Peter and John, and perceived that they were unlearned and ignorant men, they marvelled; and they took knowledge of them, that they had been with Jesus" (Acts 4:13).

A point to be made here is the remarkable result that

the boldness of Peter and John had on the rest of the brethren, for we read that, upon hearing the account of the courage of the two, "they spake the word of God with boldness" (Acts 4:31).

The same thing happened in the case of Paul in prison at Rome. The brethren waxed bold through his bonds. By his attitude toward his own suffering for preaching Christ, their daring in preaching Christ increased. Church history shows that this paradox has repeated itself many times over. We see it clearly in the following passage: "And at that time there was a great persecution against the church which was at Jerusalem; and they were all scattered abroad. . . . Therefore they that were scattered abroad went every where preaching the Word" (Acts 8:1, 4).

When the Saints at Rome saw Paul living above the circumstances, using his prison cell to preach Christ, they were challenged by his example. I wonder what God will send to us to move us out of our smugness? What circumstance must overtake us so that we will "speak the word without fear"? If you, or I, were chosen by God to suffer pain, poverty, or persecution, would we be defeated "under the circumstances," thereby discouraging the brethren, or would we live joyfully and triumphantly above the circumstances, thereby encouraging them? I feel certain that none of us is ever encouraged by our brethren who, in their own defeat, find occasion in others to criticize, to complain, and to charge for the way things are done. The Church of Jesus Christ needs more men, like Paul, who will lay hold of every circumstance as an opportunity to disseminate the gospel and increase the daring of others.

C. *Pleasure in a Greater Defense of the Gospel*

Finally, Paul was pleased: "I am set for the defence of the gospel" (Phil. 1:17).

I have heard it said that the gospel needs no defense. No doubt there is some truth to that statement, but certainly there needs to be a defense against the misrepresentations of the gospel. Paul offers an answer to this dilemma. The defense is not a quarrel with those who do not preach Christ by *my* methods and motives. There were those who were not sincere in their purpose, factiousness being their goal. But though there were men under the influence of strangely divergent motives, Paul would meet the situation by preaching Christ and rejoicing that "Christ is preached" whether in pretence or in truth. God's Word never returns fruitless in spite of the fact that we preach it only fragmentarily and sometimes factiously. The full truth should be preached with singleness and purity of purpose; nevertheless God can use any portion of His Word even when the vessel does not measure up to His standards. Frankly, I have ceased to wonder why God blesses the preaching of some of my brethren; but in more recent years, I marvel that He has blessed my own preaching, so *"I therein do rejoice, yea, and will rejoice."*

Here is a tonic to cause us to triumph amidst adversity, to make us more than conquerors in every circumstance. The main thing is that *"Christ is preached"* even if it is not always as we like. Paul's secret of his happy heart lay in the fact that he loved Christ, and it always pleased him to know that Christ's name was being spoken. We need to get our eyes off the instrument and learn to rejoice in the preaching of the truth. May God save us from the bigotry and intolerance that so frequently is attached to Christians.

Tolerance does not mean that I must compromise with error or evil. I have learned that the world has in it many different types of people. Some respond to an emotional appeal, while others give ear to a scholarly and logical presentation. The important thing for us to learn is that we should rejoice when Christ is preached, regardless of the preacher. The thing that should concern us is "the furtherance of the gospel." Remember, even though God cannot honor the motive of the messenger, He will honor and bless His word (Isaiah 55:11). Even though we cannot rejoice in the ways of some preachers, we should rejoice in the Word preached. When we are as small as to allow personal feetings to chill our enthusiasm over the preaching of Christ, we shrink our own souls and only reduce our capacity to rejoice. The best defense of the gospel is to love it sufficiently to preach it to others as opportunities arise and to rejoice in every bit of truth preached by others.

> The things that happen unto me
> Are not by chance I know—
> But because my Father's wisdom
> Has willed to have it so.
>
> For the "furtherance of the gospel"
> As a part of His great plan,
> God can use our disappointments
> And the weaknesses of man.
>
> Mrs. J. S. King

VI. PROSPECTS

For I know that this shall turn to my salvation through your prayer, and the supply of the Spirit of Jesus Christ,

According to my earnest expectation and my hope, that in nothing I shall be ashamed, but that with all boldness, as always, so now also Christ shall be magnified in my body, whether it be by life, or by death.

For to me to live is Christ, and to die is gain.

But if I live in the flesh, this is the fruit of my labour: yet what I shall choose I wot not.

For I am in a strait betwixt two, having a desire to depart, and to be with Christ; which is far better:

Nevertheless to abide in the flesh is more needful for you.

And having this confidence, I know that I shall abide and continue with you all for your furtherance and joy of faith;

That your rejoicing may be more abundant in Jesus Christ for me by my coming to you again.

Philippians 1:19-26

What are your brighest prospects and mine? What are our future expectations? I suppose we must first ask ourselves what we expect out of life. Most of us live selfishly, reaching out for those things which satisfy our natural desires. Few among us are sold out so completely to our Lord Jesus Christ that all of life, and even death itself, have only eternity's values in view. In our materialistic and grasping age it is a soul-stirring and soul-refreshing experience for me whenever I meet a selfless and self-sacrificing Christian who lives solely for Jesus Christ. Beholding such a saintly saint I am left with a holy desire to set my sights on those things that matter most.

The Apostle Paul was just that kind of saint. Undaunted by his persecution and imprisonment, his heart still undivided, Paul lays bare in this, his own spiritual autobiography, the secrets of his soul, the things he hopes for, his prospects.

A. *Dependence*

He commences with: "For I know that this shall turn to my salvation through your prayer, and the supply of the Spirit of Jesus Christ" (Phil. 1:19).

Here is a note of courageous certainty amidst conflict. Whatever good or evil came to this man of God, his prospects remained the same. There was a reason for such steadfastness: namely, divinely-given knowledge. This is the *security of the Scriptures!* Now there are some things that we do not know. The Bible says: "Ye *know not* what hour your Lord doth come" (Matt. 24:42). "*It is not for you to know* the times or the seasons, which the Father hath put in His own power" (Acts 1:7). "For we *know not* what we should pray for as we ought" (Romans 8:26). Surely we have very limited knowledge in regard to some things, but then there are other things we can know with absolute certainty. For the Christian there is no greater knowledge than that lofty statement from Paul's pen, "And *we know* that all things work together for good to them that love God, to them who are the called according to His purpose" (Rom. 8:28). The "this" in Philippians 1:19 is one of the "all things" in Romans 8:28, so that Paul can say, "I know that *this* shall turn to my salvation." Paul knew that for him everything would turn out for the best.

Much controversy has revolved around Paul's words,

"my salvation." Of course, as far as the experience of regeneration goes, Paul was fully saved. Some students of Scripture have thought that he was making reference to being saved from bodily suffering and captivity. They use Paul's words to Philemon, which were written from Rome at the time this Epistle was written, where he said: "But withal prepare me also a lodging: for I trust that through your prayers I shall be given unto you" (Philemon 22.)

This view is not impossible of accuracy when compared with other Scriptures. When Peter began to sink during his unusual episode of walking on the water, he cried: "Lord, save me" (Matt. 14:30). Certainly this prayer of Peter's, one of the shortest prayers recorded in the Bible, refers to being saved physically from death.

F. B. Meyer prefers to believe that, since the Coming again of Christ depends upon the dissemination of the gospel and the adding of members to His Church, which is His Body, Paul's experience was hastening that day because men were being saved because of it. Dr. Meyer refers to the statement in the Epistle to the Hebrews, "Unto them that look for Him shall He appear the second time without sin unto salvation" (Heb. 9:28).

I can see the possibility of either interpretation, but I must admit that whether either is correct I do not know. But of this I am certain: namely, Paul was confident that everything would turn out for the best.

In the words "through your prayers" we have a pertinent point to be pondered. This is *the supplication of the saints*. Earlier in the Epistle Paul wrote: "I pray" (1:9). Now he takes it for granted that they are praying also. In almost all of his writings Paul makes mention of a mutual fellowship and dependence through prayer. "I make mention of you always in *my prayers*. . . . Now I beseech you, brethren, for the Lord Jesus Christ's sake, and for the love of the Spirit, that ye strive together with me in *your prayers* to God for me" (Rom. 1:9; 15:30). "I . . . cease not to give thanks for you, making mention of you in *my prayers*. . . . Finally, my brethren . . . *Praying always . . . for me*" (Eph. 1:16; 6:10, 18-19). "And this *I pray,* that your love may abound. . . . I know that this shall turn to my salvation through *your prayer*" (Phil. 1:9, 19). *"Making mention of you in our prayers*. . . . Night and day. . . . *Brethren, pray for us"* (1 Thess. 1:2; 3:10; 5:25). "Wherefore also *we pray always for you*. . . . Finally, brethren, *pray for us"* (2 Thess. 1:11; 3:1).

It is hardly possible for us to conceive the value and importance Paul placed upon mutual dependence in prayer. Certainly he was counting heaviest upon God Himself, but his positive declaration in the words "I know" was based, in part, at least, upon the prayers of the saints. He believed in the power and effectiveness of prayer. Did you notice the order in the expression of the interdependency upon prayer? In each instance Paul prays *for them* before he requests prayer *for himself.* This is as it should be. Why should I expect that others are praying for me when I am not interested sufficiently in others to pray for them?

It is this double side of our prayer life that makes prayer so sweet a fellowship. How trite and unworthy, sometimes, the request, "Pray for me." Do we really expect the arm of God to move in our behalf merely because we asked someone else to pray for us while we ourselves are living prayerless lives? None save the man of prayer, who knows somewhat the power of prayer, could say: "I know that this shall turn to my salvation through your prayers." Paul prayed for others and relied strongly on the prayers of others.

As a pastor I cannot put too much stress on the need for the intercession of the Church. God must raise up among us more men and women who will give themselves to intercessory prayer. More time should be given to prayer and less time to entertainment, sports, and social life. Every human need, every case of backsliding is a call to prayer. We see it exemplified in the early church. "Peter therefore was kept in prison: but prayer was made without ceasing of the church unto God for him" (Acts 12:5).

Prayer is the link that will keep our hearts knit closely together in the bonds of the gospel. Get the Church to its knees and revival blessing will remain with us. We need and depend upon each other, and the throne of grace is a commonplace among us. We need the supplication of the saints.

Paul knew further that his present circumstance would result in his spiritual profit through *"the supply of the Spirit of Jesus Christ."* He was not depending merely upon the prayers of the saints, but also upon the provision of the Spirit. The human and the divine were both essential.

The word "supply" suggests the idea of a grant or provision, in the sense of giving what is necessary for assistance or help. The Holy Spirit has a ministry to all believers, the supply being inexhaustible, and in all His varied ministrations He will meet our needs, however many we have. He will supply and support; He will render assistance. To this end He was sent into the world that we might enjoy His *companionship* (John 14:16) and His *counsel* (John 14:26), that we might have *courage* for witnessing (John 15:26-27), and that there might be *conviction* in our ministry (John 16:7). He searches out the deep things of God (1 Cor. 2:9-10). He prays for us when we feel we must pray but cannot find words to pray as we ought (Rom. 8:26). His is a bountiful supply. "The supply of the Spirit of Jesus Christ" might be translated "The bounteous supply which the Spirit gives through Jesus Christ." Paul had drawn from that divine resource so freely that he could write: "But my God shall supply all your need according to His riches in glory by Christ Jesus" (Phil. 4:19).

The Holy Spirit both supplies and supports spiritual life. We are saved by the Spirit (Titus 3:5), and strengthened by the Spirit (Eph. 3:16). In the regenerate soul He dwells so that all who are in Christ can draw upon His bounteous supply. How much we need the continuous supply that flows from Him! And remember, God never cuts off the supply from His children. When the rivers of living water cease to flow, somewhere in our lives we have caused the stoppage.

How much do we know of the supply of the Spirit that causes one to rejoice in tribulation, to rise triumphantly above every circumstance, and to bear a good witness for our Lord? There is a well-timed assistance for every emergency supplied by the blessed Spirit of God. We need the security of the Scriptures, the supplication of the saints, and the supply of the Spirit. Keep all supply lines open. Learn to depend upon the Word, prayer, and the Spirit's power. What blessed and assuring prospects!

B. *Decision*

Every Christian has become one because he made a personal decision to receive the salvation offered to all men in Jesus Christ. Becoming saved is an individual and personal matter. It is not possible for the faith of one to save another; else few, if any, would be lost. Men cannot be saved en masse, but rather singly and individually as each for himself believes on the Lord Jesus Christ.

This same pattern necessarily follows in the experiences of men after they become saved. The personal decision that one Christian may make in his relations to Jesus Christ must be made for himself alone. Such a decision may influence others, but it cannot be transferred to them.

The Apostle Paul made some personal decisions that were among life's choicest. Those were his prospects, the things for which he lived. Possibly none surpasses that which he expressed in our present passage: "According to my earnest expectation and my hope, that in nothing I shall be ashamed, but that with all boldness, as always, so now also Christ shall be magnified in my body, whether it be by life, or by death" (Phil. 1:20).

What is your most earnest expectation and hope? What is mine? One might think that with Paul it would be his release from prison or relief from suffering for Christ. I am afraid that with some of us it would be just that. Paul's prospects were the highest, reaching into eternity, and always they were related to the glory of Jesus Christ.

His "earnest expectation and hope" were his forward look. As one would watch intently with neck stretched and head tilted in the direction of the approaching visit of the highest official in the land, so the great apostle set himself to do something. What was it? Facing a crisis which could ultimate in his being beheaded, this servant of the Lord was determined, as he said, *"that in nothing I shall be ashamed."*

With head erect, Paul decided that in the end, when he stood before Jesus Christ, he would not be put to shame through failing as Christ's witness. A wise decision indeed! Who among us has not at one time or another been put to shame when our sin was detected and exposed? Adam tried to hide himself, not because he had sinned, but because he knew himself to be exposed (naked). He said: "I was afraid, because I was naked; and I hid myself" (Gen. 3:10). We are like Adam in that we fear the shame, not for our wrongdoing itself but for being detected in our sin.

About four years before this prison experience, Paul wrote: "For we must all appear before the judgment seat of Christ; that every one may receive the things done in his body, according to that he hath done, whether it be good or bad" (2 Cor. 5:10).

The word "appear" means *to be manifest without disguise*. This was an incentive that prompted Paul in his labor. His ambitions and prospects were guided by the fact that he would one day face his Lord, and he wanted to be "accepted of Him" (2 Cor. 5:9). Paul, like every believer, was already accepted *in* Him, but now he lived and labored to be accepted *of* Him. Our goals, ambitions, and prospects will determine largely the kind of lives we live. No one, who has ever considered seriously the reality of that coming day when we must be made manifest without disguise before the Judgment Seat of Christ, would fail to live so as not to be ashamed in that critical hour. "And now, little children, abide in Him; that, when He shall appear, we may have confidence, and not be ashamed before Him at His coming" (1 John 2:28).

This was Paul's prospect and it was founded on a great decision. Is it yours and mine? There is a strong admonition here for us all. Our lives may not be so emphatically marked out for distinction and renown as was Paul's, but for every believer there will be a day of reckoning. The Judgment Seat of Christ is not to determine whether or not we are Christians, but rather to bring to light the character of our practical Christianity. This is all very solemn and it should inspire us to hold our heads erect in anticipation of Christ's Coming and to live and labor so as not to be ashamed. What are our prospects? Is our outlook filled with glowing confidence? If not, then decide with Paul, "that in nothing I shall be ashamed."

C. *Dedication*

Christ shall be magnified in my body, whether it be by life, or by death.

Phil. 1:20

Notice, *first*, the *value* of magnifying Christ. Here the word "magnify" means "to make great, to enlarge." Someone may ask: "How can I add anything to Christ's greatness? Can an impotent creature add to the Creator's omnipotence? Can a contribution out of my poverty add to His unlimited wealth? How can I make Christ great?" I can only say that we can magnify Him in that sphere of the unbelieving world where He is minimized; we can glorify Him in the presence of those who are blind to His glory; we can display His grace to those who have never seen and known it.

Let us face the fact that we occupy a small portion of the universe where the greatness and glory of sinful men and women excel, in the minds of the masses, the greatness and glory of our Lord Jesus Christ. For filthy lucre the moving picture industry magnifies those men and women who attract the largest crowds to the ticket window. In the sports and show business the stars are magnified who make the best box office attraction. In all of this the Son of God is relegated well nigh to obscurity. Someone must make Him gloriously conspicuous! The cry of the Psalmist needs to be sounded to Christians everywhere—"O magnify the Lord with me" (Psalm 34:3).

The experience of Mary should be ours, when she said: "My soul doth magnify the Lord" (Luke 1:46). John recognized what each of us must come to see: namely, "He [Christ] must increase, but I must decrease" (John 3:30).

Next, Paul sets forth the *vehicle* for magnifying Christ —"my body." Please observe with the greatest of care that Paul is not magnifying his body but rather Christ in his body. The human heart has never risen above the pagan, lustful urge to glorify the human body. One week prior to the time of this writing, a column in the newspaper, announcing the arrival of a certain movie actress, had as the lead statement in its article, "The Body Comes to Town." It is not uncommon to see today, in all walks of life, attempts to glorify these dying and decaying bodies of ours. Now there is no sin in our giving proper expression to a wholesome appreciation of natural beauty and God-given physical attractiveness, but even in this there is need for exercising restraint.

J. H. Pickford writes: "The unseen Life and Love needs a screen upon which to reflect His image: That screen is our body. The Lord Jesus Christ needed a body in which to fulfil His covenant pledges. If spirit were enough to bring salvation to man, Christ need not have come to earth, but could have suffered on a spiritual cross on a spiritual hill, unseen and unknown. Apart from the body, it was not possible to communicate His love and life to the world. His body gave Him the capacity to live, to suffer, and to die as Man for men." "Wherefore when He cometh into the world, He saith, Sacrifice and offering Thou wouldest not, but a body hast Thou prepared Me" (Heb. 10:5).

Now His body is no longer here in which to glorify the Father, but before He returned to Heaven He purchased some bodies to carry on this great work while Christ was yet on the earth. "Philip saith unto Him, Lord, shew us the Father, and it sufficeth us. Jesus saith unto him . . . he that hath seen Me hath seen the Father" (John 14:8-9).

A part of God's redemptive process was to prepare many bodies in which Christ might be magnified. My brethren, our bodies are for this very purpose. "What? know ye not that your body is the temple of the Holy Ghost which is in you, which ye have of God, and ye are not your own? For ye are bought with a price: therefore glorify God in your body, and in your spirit, which are God's" (1 Cor. 6:19-20).

This was both Paul's declaration for the entire Body of Christ and his desire for his own body in particular. There is no telling to what extent the blessing of God will come to men if only He can get hold of our bodies. "I beseech you therefore, brethren, by the mercies of God, that ye present your bodies a living sacrifice, holy, acceptable unto God, which is your reasonable service" (Rom. 12:1).

God wants to possess our bodies. What are we doing with them? Are we decorating them to draw attention to ourselves? Are our bodies given to sinful practices and the seeking of worldly pleasures?

Once upon a time four young men dedicated their bodies to God in order to magnify their God. They refused to eat and drink the world's fare (Dan. 1:8). The ruling monarch of Babylon condemned three of them to a fiery furnace and later had the fourth cast into a den of lions. But God protected the bodies of His own possessions and through those yielded bodies He was magnified. "Then Nebuchadnezzar spake, and said, Blessed be the God of Shadrach, Meshach, and Abednego, who hath sent His angel, and delivered His servants that trusted in Him, and have changed the king's word, and yielded their bodies, that they might not serve nor worship any god, except their own God" (Dan. 3:28).

Have you ever dedicated your body, yielded it so completely, that Christ is magnified in its members? Guy H. King wrote about this and said: "Christ magnified in the body—magnified by lips that bear happy testimony to Him; magnified by hands employed in His service; magnified by feet only too happy to go on His errands; magnified by knees happily bent in prayer; magnified by shoulders happy to bear one another's burdens."

The same writer further pointed out two kinds of magnification. There is the *microscopic*, that makes the little seem big. This we do not think of here since there is nothing little about our Lord. Then there is the *telescopic* that makes the really big loom bigger. The star may appear as a dot in the distance, but the telescope will bring it out in truer proportions. It brings the distant near.

Christ is so distant from the world of our day. The body of each Christian must be as a mighty telescope, bringing to the sinner a sense of His real nearness. Oh, that our blessed Lord might be magnified in our bodies!

Finally, Paul speaks of the *vantage* of magnifying Christ! So desirous and so determined was the apostle that Christ be magnified in his body, he dedicated his body to that end "whether it be by life, or by death" (Phil. 1:20). He holds no mental reservations in his determination. While most of us would be troubled about our existence, Paul was exercised about Christ's exaltation, so much that he was willing and ready to go the limit for his Lord. If it pleases God to allow him to live awhile longer on this earth, he will magnify Christ by his life.

On the other hand, if God chooses to remove him from this earthly scene through death, then he is determined to exalt Christ in his death. Even as Christ's body gave Him the capacity to live and die for us, so Paul's body presented to him an opportunity to live or die so as to glorify the Lord Jesus. This was the controlling principle in the life of the great apostle—*"as always, so now."* It was no mere emotional stir born in the excitement of a moment of pumped-up enthusiasm, but the product of daily deliberation and decisive determination.

But what advantage is there in making such a decision? Paul answers this question: "For to me to live is Christ, and to die is gain" (Phil. 1:21).

For Paul, Christ was the real reason for living. The man

who lives for Christ has everything to live for. There is great advantage in this.

But what is life to you and me? For us what does it mean to live? If we were honest, we would confess that life to some of us is to be recognized by others, or to become rich, or to enjoy recreation, or to retire in comfort. But there is no vantage in living thus, for then death would be a great disappointment. Life is worth living only when we live for Christ, for only He can give meaning and purpose to life. Dr. R. L. Laurin suggests that when we remove from the sentence the words "Christ is gain" with its corrective qualifying word "and," all that remains is, "For me to live is to die." This just about describes life for those who have lived to gratify the lusts of the flesh. They have lived to die, and because they lived selfishly, they gained nothing through living. For Paul, life had but one meaning and one interpretation. He lived for Christ. Apart from Christ, life was purposeless.

He who lives for Christ will discover that death is gain. The Christian who makes Christ the whole purpose and pursuit of life never looks upon death as a misfortune or something to be feared. He has no hesitation in concluding that "to die is gain." How did Paul look upon dying? It was "to depart." This metaphor suggests the idea of loosing the moorings to set sail. Many a weather-beaten, sea-weary mariner has looked forward to his last ocean voyage and final retirement to the haven of his heart's desire. That final voyage brings no regret to the mariner who has given himself selflessly and sacrificially to his duties. Even so, death is never dreaded but rather desired by the one who has lived for Christ.

My good friend Dr. Andrew Telford and I stepped into

an elevator in Augusta, Georgia. Ever alert and desirous of saying a word for his Lord, Dr. Telford asked the elevator operator, "Will your last trip be up or down?" I watched attentively for the reaction. It was sad, for it was obvious that the man was not prepared to "depart." He was not ready to loose the moorings and set sail for the final voyage. But Paul was. He testified: "For I am now ready to be offered, and the time of my departure is at hand" (2 Tim. 4:6).

Oh brethren, are we ready to depart? After all, we know that the earth is not our permanent dwelling place. Saints in every dispensation should know that their relationship to this earth is a transient one. Of Abraham it is written: "By faith he sojourned in the land of promise, as in a strange country, dwelling in tabernacles with Isaac and Jacob, the heirs with him of the same promise: For he looked for a city which hath foundations, whose builder and maker is God" (Heb. 11:9-10).

Of all Old Testament saints, who believed God, it is said: "These all died in faith, not having received the promises, but having seen them afar off, and were persuaded of them, and embraced them, and confessed that they were strangers and pilgrims on the earth" (Heb. 11:13).

The word "pilgrim" is used metaphorically of all those to whom Heaven is home and who are but sojourners on earth. Peter wrote to the "strangers," and said: "Peter, an apostle of Jesus Christ, to the strangers scattered throughout Pontus, Galatia, Cappadocia, Asia, and Bithynia. . . . Dearly beloved, I beseech you as strangers and pilgrims, abstain from fleshly lusts, which war against the soul" (1 Peter 1:1; 2:11).

Christians are foreigners here, and earth is our temporary residence. Earth is not our home. Actually, we are not citizens of earth. The word "citizens" is used metaphorically in a spiritual sense of the Christian's heavenly relationship and destiny. "Now therefore ye are no more strangers and foreigners, but fellowcitizens with the saints, and of the household of God" (Eph. 2:19). "For our citizenship is in Heaven; whence also we wait for a Saviour, the Lord Jesus Christ (Phil. 3:20 R. V.).

When we committed our lives to Jesus Christ, we pledged allegiance to another monarch of another country. Realizing that we are here for only a short time in order that we may glorify Him, we dare not drive our stakes too deeply. But it is to be feared that too many professing Christians are not ready for the detachment, not willing for the weighing of the anchor.

Now I am not suggesting that we are to welcome death as death. Contrariwise, it is natural to shrink from it. But looked at in the light of eternity, death is a perfectly glorious thing, for it is but the unloosing from the trials, disappointments, bodily suffering, and heartaches of this earthly experience.

Little wonder Paul was eager to set sail! His departure meant that he would "be with Christ; which is far better" (1:23). Now death is not the Christian's hope. The Coming of the Lord to receive us is our hope. Yet if death comes to the believer, it cannot separate him from Christ. Death is still gain since it takes him "to be with Christ." "Therefore we are always confident, knowing that, whilst we are at home in the body, we are absent from the Lord: (For we walk by faith, not by sight:) We are confident, I say, and willing rather to be absent from the body, and to be present with the Lord" (2 Cor. 5:6-8).

Are you ready for the voyage, whether by the Rapture or by death? For Paul the departure was no unwelcome tragedy. It was no cold thrust into the unknown. Recently the newspapers made much of the marriage of the world's richest man. It made me wonder what percentage of wealthy professing Christians are possessed of the holy desire to depart? On this I dare not speculate. I only know that my own heart, at this time, is possessed of the desire so to live my life for my Lord that death will be gain.

Someone may ask, "Are our friends on earth to be taken lightly? Are they to mean nothing at all to us?" I believe we can find an answer, in part at least, in the verses before us. It seems as if Paul faced a dilemma in this very thing. Hear him say, "What I shall choose I wot not. For I am in a straight betwixt two." He was torn between two desires. On the one hand, he wanted to stay on to minister and see the fruit of his labor. The saints needed that ministry, for the apostle adds: "Nevertheless to abide in the flesh is more needful for you" (Phil. 1:24).

On the other hand, the veteran warrior for Christ was a bit homesick for Heaven, where he would be with Jesus. He was not fed up with life and its labors. He lived to see sinners saved and saints strengthened in their faith. But then, not even earth's sweetest ties in a lifetime can compare with the first moments "with Christ." How rich and wondrous will be the soul's communion with the Lord in that day! If I live in the flesh and continue to serve Christ, it will be worth my while; but if I depart to be with Christ, that will be the best yet.

Having clearly before us a knowledge of Paul's desire: namely, "to depart, and to be with Christ," we see him now weighing carefully the needs of the brethren and therefore deciding that he is willing to remain and serve. "Nevertheless to abide in the flesh is more needful for you. And having this confidence, I know that I shall abide and continue with you all for your furtherance and joy of faith" (Phil. 1:24-25).

Writing by inspiration, Paul doubtless received assurance from God that he would be released from his prison chains to go forth and serve (1:25). He was unselfish. If others could be helped through his efforts, he would not shirk his responsibilities and thrust them upon others merely to realize his own desires. He could forego his own desires for that which is "more needful" for others. God had shown His servant that the divine will for him was longer life and a larger labor for the furtherance (progress) and joy of others.

Now the conclusion of the matter is this: There is a vantage for others through Paul's magnifying Christ in his body: "That your rejoicing may be more abundant in Jesus Christ for me by my coming to you again" (Phil. 1:26).

How far Paul's anticipation was realized we do not know. In his account in the Acts, Luke closes with the mention of Paul's imprisonment in Rome. From his pastoral Epistles it would seem that Paul was released from this first imprisonment in Rome and that he did undertake further travel and testimony for Christ. At any rate, the apostle was no dreamer, sitting idly by and speculating about Heaven. His views of the life to come were closely tied to the needs about him. May God grant that all of us may have more joy in our labors, thereby increasing the rejoicing of others. Make up your mind today to lay aside your personal preference, and for the glory of Christ and the sake of others, magnify Christ in your body.

VII. PLEADING

Only let your conversation be as it becometh the gospel of Christ: that whether I come and see you, or else be absent, I may hear of your affairs, that ye stand fast in one spirit, with one mind striving together for the faith of the gospel;

And in nothing terrified by your adversaries; which is to them an evident token of perdition, but to you of salvation, and that of God.

For unto you it is given in the behalf of Christ, not only to believe on Him, but also to suffer for His sake;

Having the same conflict which ye saw in me, and now hear to be in me.

Philippians 1:27-30

Until now Paul has been writing, for the most part, in the first person, the Epistle being chiefly autobiographical, the one exception being his prayer in verses 9-11. Here the tenor of his message shifts to an application of spiritual truths to his readers and hearers. This is a missing note in present-day ministry and needs to be revived. Preaching and teaching in the abstract and in generalities to no one in particular does not build strong Christians. Truth must be applied. It must appeal to the conscience of the hearer.

Paul commences his plea with the use of the important word "conversation." It is not conversation in the sense of words, but of works; not of language, but of life. The word "conversation" means *citizenship* as in 3:20, carrying with it the clear connotation of one's manner of life. The Christian's manner of life was to be such as to be a credit to the gospel of Jesus Christ. He who is saved by the gospel is expected to live a life worthy of the gospel.

The word "becometh" is an interesting one. We often hear it said that someone's clothing does or does not *become* him. What is meant is that if the color and cut of a garment enhance the face and personality of the person wearing it, then the garment is becoming. This is exactly what Paul has in mind here: "That they may adorn the doctrine of God our Saviour in all things" (Titus 2:10).

Christian behavior in Scripture is likened to garments. After one believes the gospel, there are some things he must "put off" and others he must "put on." "But now ye also *put off* all these; anger, wrath, malice, blasphemy, filthy communication out of your mouth. Lie not one to another, seeing that ye have put off the old man with his deeds; And have put on the new man, which is renewed in knowledge after the image of Him that created him. . . . *Put on* therefore, as the elect of God, holy and beloved, bowels of mercies, kindness, humbleness of mind, meekness, longsuffering; Forbearing one another, and forgiving one another, if any man have a quarrel against any: even as Christ forgave you, so also do ye. And above all these things put on charity, which is the bond of perfectness" (Col. 3:8-10, 12-14).

Do your spiritual garments become your Christian profession? Are you as concerned about adorning the gospel by your manner of life as you are your body by the clothing you wear? Do you spend more time, effort, and money on adorning the gospel than you do on adorning your body? Our manner of life as Christians either helps or hinders the gospel, it either recommends the truth to others or else makes the truth repulsive.

Paul is here pleading for gospel-worthy Christians who will carry on for Jesus Christ without the prop of the apostle's presence. He is saying to them, "Let your manner of life be consistent with the truth of the gospel *whether I come and see you, or else be absent.*" The desire in the heart of every true pastor is to feed those in the assembly so they can stand alone with God upon His Word. It is a grief to any man of God to have his people take the attitude that they just cannot get along without him. Personally, I am never flattered by those who bemoan my absence as though the blessing of God leaves my local assembly when I am away. If every Christian's manner of life becomes the gospel, there never need be any fear when the pastor is elsewhere. The church at Philippi felt it owed its existence to Paul, thus they were in great danger of leaning upon him rather than upon Christ. If they depended on Paul, or on any man, their experience was borrowed and they were parasites. If they were truly Christ's, they would look to Him for needed strength and wisdom. So whether the apostle is with them or absent from them, he hopes to hear a good report of their "affairs."

A. *A Plea to Stand*

First, "*Stand* fast in one spirit, with one mind." The basis for this whole plea is the fact that there is a war on. The saints are engaged in a great conflict. Paul tells them the battle is with "your adversaries" (1:28), and he adds that it is "the same conflict which ye saw in me" (1:30). He, along with all saints, had been put in trust with the gospel (1 Thess. 2:4), and the gospel had, and still has, its enemies. He had exercised himself in the "confirmation

of the gospel" (1:7), "the furtherance of the gospel"
he pleads with his brethren to live "as it becometh the
(1:12), "the defence of the gospel" (1:7, 17), and now
gospel" (1:27). Because the adversaries are many and
mighty, the saints will have to "stand fast in one spirit,
with one mind."

Our ecumenical times do not allow us to "stand" for much of anything lest we offend others who do not agree with us. We have been taught that to win friends and influence people we ought not to be dogmatic and unbending. "After all," said a well-known Protestant minister, "there is some good in every man's religion, so why should I insist that my way is right?" Obviously, his way is not right; but Christ's is. Hence those who believe the gospel of Christ are to adorn that gospel by their lives and "stand fast in one spirit, with one mind." Merrill C. Tenney writes: "In this common conviction and cause lies the foundation of a true ecumenicity. Fellowship in the faith and in the propagation of the gospel produces unity."

Our standing together must be "in one spirit, with one mind." I am not certain in my own mind whether or not the "one spirit" here refers to the Holy Spirit, the one Spirit present in all the members of the Body of Christ. I see in it a unity of spirit and purpose imparted and controlled by the Holy Spirit. The "one mind" has reference to a unified purpose and program with no divided opinions. They were to stand unitedly because the adversaries would attempt to divide and destroy. In his Ephesian Epistle Paul exhorted the saints: "I therefore, the prisoner of the Lord, beseech you that ye walk worthy of the vocation wherewith ye are called, With all lowliness and meekness, with longsuffering, forbearing one another in love; Endeavouring to keep the unity of the Spirit in the bond of peace" (Eph. 4:1-3).

The word "keep" here means to guard. Believers are one in Christ, and knowing that the enemy's design is to split the ranks and thereby destroy a witness for Christ, each of us must go all out to guard that oneness. I know of nothing that mars a gospel testimony as does disunity among God's people caused by self-seeking. Nothing is more harmful to the unsaved than to discover division among Christians. If Satan can disrupt the ranks of God's children, he has won a great victory. He knows the truth of our Lord's statement: "Every city or house divided against itself shall not stand" (Matt. 12:25).

The local assembly needs to maintain a single front. Our Lord prayed for His own, "That they all may be one . . . that the world may believe" (John 17:21). To stand fast in one spirit, with one mind, means to face the opposition unitedly. Unity is essential in the home, in business, and in the Church. We must stand firm and upright in perfect oneness. F. A. Noble has said: "A church in which the sentiment of unity has been displaced by the bitterness of mutual ill will might as well go at once into the hands of a receiver. The days of its usefulness and prosperity are at an end." Oh, beloved brethren, let us stand hand to hand, heart to heart, and shoulder to shoulder.

B. *A Plea to Strive*

"Striving together for the faith of the gospel." "Striving" is the translation of a word used of a contest and means "to contend." The idea of cooperation is here, suggesting that a group of athletes cooperate as a team against an opposing team. Here the "adversaries," Satan's team, are matched against the Church of Christ. The contest calls for teamwork, a pulling together. A football team gets its signal, and then every man on that team strives together to reach the goal. If the Church would strive together in one spirit, with one mind, in carrying out God's program, as does a team in games of sport and skill, the world would soon know about our Lord Jesus Christ and His salvation. Our efforts together must show the teamwork of the training and discipline of the Holy Spirit.

In my contacts among various assemblies that meet in the name of our Lord Jesus Christ, I find a great need for the consideration of the very truths Paul is teaching here. Instead of striving together as a team against a common foe, many saints today bicker among themselves. The striving is not together against the adversaries but rather against each other. Because of this, the very thing, which we should be striving together to promote, suffers.

We are to strive together *"for the faith of the gospel."* This means the whole body of inspired and revealed truth as placed within the confines of the Book we know as the Bible. This is God's full and final revelation and the object of Satan's most bitter attacks. Concerning "the faith" Jude wrote: "Beloved, when I gave all diligence to write unto you of the common salvation, it was needful for me to write unto you, and exhort you that ye should earnestly contend for *the faith* which was once delivered unto the saints" (Jude 3).

Our program is the propagation, and thus, the preservation, of *the faith*. It is our historic Christian faith. In our day of departure from *the faith* we must go all out in guarding the unity of the Spirit that our united strength shall be used to spread *the faith* of the gospel. This objective is so supremely worthwhile one might conclude that believers would permit nothing whatever to hinder the carrying of it out. Since unity assures us of added strength, let us unite to move forward in victory.

Such a task calls for boldness, fearlessness, and courage. Paul continues his plea: "And in nothing terrified by your adversaries: which is to them an evident token of perdition, but to you of salvation, and that of God" (Phil. 1:28).

This mighty servant of the Lord, bound in a Roman prison, is telling the believers not to allow the opponents of the gospel to frighten or to intimidate them. We can in nowise concede to the enemy, for such steadfastness on our part is at the same time a sure sign of their doom. Our banding together for the faith of the gospel shows the enemies of Christ the futility of their efforts to oppose Him. On the other hand, the oneness and steadfastness of the saints assures them of a God-given victory. If we persevere, we shall be preserved to carry on the struggle to a glorious and triumphant climax. Never be afraid of the enemies of the gospel: "Greater is He that is in you, than he that is in the world" (1 John 4:4).

How disturbing to the enemy is the steadfastness of the saints!

C. *A Plea to Suffer*

Paul concludes his plea by reminding them that they are called by God to *suffer:* "For unto you it is given in the behalf of Christ, not only to believe on Him, but also to suffer for His sake" (Phil. 1:29).

This verse simply tells us that the privilege has been bestowed upon us to suffer in the place of Christ. We know it is not possible for any sinner to share in our Lord's expiatory sufferings which He experienced at Calvary. But we can suffer for righteousness' sake, even as He suffered. Faith in Christ and suffering for Christ are inseparable experiences. The very fact that a man identifies himself with Jesus Christ will result in his suffering for his Lord. Jesus said: "If they have persecuted Me, they will also persecute you" (John 15:20).

Paul wrote a little later: "Yea, and all that will live godly in Christ Jesus shall suffer persecution" (2 Tim. 3:12).

To believe in Christ in our day means the very opposite of hardship and suffering. It has come to mean that the believer now has a place in a church pew where he can sit snugly and smugly. But when the child of God takes his place in the battle against evil, the devil will see to it that he has plenty of opposition. Paul speaks of such suffering as a favor granted of God. Actually it is a part of the *grace* of God bestowed on Christians when we are called to share the sufferings of Christ. The apostle realized this when called upon to suffer. "And they departed from the presence of the council, rejoicing that they were counted worthy to suffer shame for His name" (Acts 5:41).

Suffering may differ today in meaning from its meaning in the earlier days of the Church. By that I mean that it may not mean bodily torment, imprisonment, starvation, and even a torturous death, but it will always be the price one pays when he sincerely and uncompromisingly identifies himself with Jesus Christ. To stand, to strive, to suffer always has been the experience of those who love the Lord Jesus Christ. It was Paul's personal experience when he wrote this Epistle, and it is his plea to each of us.

VIII. PLEADING (Continued)

> If there be therefore any consolation in Christ, if any comfort of love, if any fellowship of the Spirit, if any bowels and mercies,
>
> Fulfil ye my joy, that ye be likeminded, having the same love, being of one accord, of one mind.
>
> Let nothing be done through strife or vainglory; but in lowliness of mind let each esteem other better than themselves.
>
> Look not every man on his own things, but every man also on the things of others.
>
> Philippians 2:1-4

The apostle's message in the opening verses of the second chapter of Philippians is closely related to the closing appeal in chapter one. The kinship between the two passages is obvious. The opening words of this chapter, "If there be therefore . . ." are intimately connected with what has gone before. Here Paul is pressing on in his appeal for unity and humility. We have included these two passages in our outline under the general heading, *Pleading*.

The appeal is fourfold, each commencing with the words "If any":

If there be *any* consolation in Christ . . .
If any comfort of love . . .
If any fellowship of the Spirit . . .
If any bowels and mercies

Here are four reasons why the members of the Church should live in close harmony. Now the "if" does not imply that there might not be any consolation in Christ, comfort of love, fellowship of the Spirit, bowels and mercies. The four things mentioned in verse one are not hypothetical; they are four existing facts. The word "if" can be translated "since" or "in view of the fact." The basis of Paul's appeal for unity among these believers is this fourfold experience:

A. *Consolation*

"If there be therefore any *consolation* in Christ." If they had experienced anything of the gentle encouragement of Christ, and most certainly they had, then that experience should challenge them to live together in a state of harmony. What Christ had done for them, and for us, should be an incentive to peaceful and purposeful pursuits. The very fact that believers are one in Christ should have a binding effect upon us. In the Body of Christ there is no room for schism, cliques, isolated groups, and divisions. Instead, let us act as though the ministry of Christ in our behalf were a blessed reality.

B. *Comfort*

"If any *comfort* of love." If the love of God had been truly shed abroad in their hearts, comforting them, it would promote among them harmonized relations. The tenderness of God, as experienced in His love for His children, should urge them to live together in a spirit of unity. Since God loved them enough to sacrifice His son for them they should love one another with that same sacrificial love. There is no internal strife where God's love is appreciated. The moment Christ ceases to be real to us, we lose our affection for others. Paul is saying: "If love has any hold on you, then be like-minded."

C. *Communion*

"If any fellowship of the Spirit." As Christians, they surely had known somewhat of the communion of the Holy Ghost. Now they are to be willing to walk in the fellowship of the Spirit, not in selfishness and pride. If there is any one reason why there should be unity, it is found right here: "For by [in] one Spirit are we all baptized into one body, whether we be Jews or Gentiles, whether we be bond or free; and have been all made to drink into one Spirit" (1 Cor. 12:13). The word "fellowship" means a joint partnership. As members of one body, indwelt by the same Holy Spirit, there must be unity and like-mindedness. Every believer is a temple of the Holy Spirit. "What? know ye not that your body is the temple of the Holy Ghost which is in you, which ye have of God, and ye are not your own?" (1 Cor. 6:19). His indwelling makes us copartners with Him, hence with each other. This spiritual union demands Spirit-sharing among us.

D. *Compassion*

"If any bowels and mercies." Paul seems to be saying, "If there is anything to your Christian experience, then there is an impulse of sympathy for others." Such compassion is not merely a humanitarian kindness and sympathy which results in philanthropic deeds. Paul is digging under the surface of the mere shallow, superficial appeal that is so common in religion today. He is calling upon all that is tender and compassionate in their new nature to come now to the fore and make for unity among them.

Having given fourfold basis for his appeal for unity and humility in verse one, he sets alongside of that *appeal* a practical *approach* for its accomplishment in verse two. It is a tender and gracious appeal set forth in the spirit of love and longing.

> Fulfil ye my joy, that ye be likeminded, having the same love, being of one accord, of one mind.
>
> Phil. 2:2

He seems to be saying, "You have caused my heart to rejoice before (1:4), now fill my cup of rejoicing to the brim. Do this favor for me." He then proceeds with a fourfold approach.

First, " be likeminded." They are to set before them the same goals and contemplate the same things and be unanimous in their decisions. True Christian unity is like-mindedness, thinking the same things.

Secondly, "having the same love." Here unity commences. Dr. R. L. Laurin emphasizes love, rather than knowledge, as the starting place if there is to be unity. He cites the mighty leaders of the Reformation as men of great intellect and unfaltering courage but failing in their love, thus producing a group of quibbling theologians. There must be unity of affection for God's Word, God's work, God's workmen, and most certainly we must share God's love for the world of lost mankind.

Thirdly, "being of one accord." The hearts of believers in every local assembly must be knit together and mutually constrained by the same urge and desire. Any group inspired by the same love will have a common accord.

Fourthly, "of one mind." Four times in five verses this word "mind" occurs. The idea is not so much that of one's intellectual apprehension as of one's mental attitude. It is not the difference of viewpoint that makes for disunity among us, but rather a wrong attitude toward others whose viewpoint differs from our own. If we were more willing to face the problem from our brother's viewpoint, there would be fewer differences among us.

It is not to be expected that Christians will see eye to eye on every detail. Our thoughts and actions are largely influenced by heredity, environment, and education; hence it is well nigh impossible to find a group of Christians who will see everything from the same viewpoint. How then shall we dissolve our differences and solve our problems? Paul gives a satisfactory solution in verses three and four:

> Let nothing be done through strife or vainglory; but in lowliness of mind let each esteem other better than themselves.
>
> Phil. 2:3

At no time and under no condition should believers strive among themselves. Strife, or contention, is an expression of enmity and always results in faction. Disputing and quarreling ought never to exist among brethren in Christ. "And the servant of the Lord must not strive; but be gentle unto all men, apt to teach, patient" (2 Tim. 2:24).

After approaching the problem from the negative point of view, Paul now adds a positive approach:

. . . but in lowliness of mind let each esteem other better than themselves.

Phil. 2:3

True unity will be destroyed where self-esteem prevails rather than a higher esteem for others. Whenever the dominant note in any Christian group is selflessness and self-forgetfulness, unity will take the place of factiousness. I have seen the spirit of self-esteem and self-importance break up more than one fine fellowship. Each of us must see our own insignificance, have a modest opinion of ourselves, and count our fellow men better and more excellent than we consider ourselves to be. I know of no other way to carry out God's program with success apart from denying self and waging an all-out warfare against the proud thoughts of self. Spiritual unity is needed in the church today. May God help each of us to pay the price to attain it. Let us do away at once with all self-seeking. Paul learned by hard experience that he had to bring his old self-life with its empty pride to the Cross. He said: "But God forbid that I should glory, save in the cross of our Lord Jesus Christ, by whom the world is crucified unto me, and I unto the world" (Gal. 6:14).

And now the apostle gives his final word in his plea before turning to the perfect Pattern of genuine humility.

Look not every man on his own things, but every man also on the things of others.

Phil. 2:4

The selfish and self-seeking man looks out for himself. He is taken up with his own interests. But the Christian, for the sake of unity, is exhorted to look not on his own interests, but on the interests of others. It is a part of our fallen human nature to suppose that life's greatest happiness can be found in man's satisfying his own desire. If each board or committee in the church, each department or individual class in the Sunday school, were to insist on separate group advantages, nothing would be gained beyond strife and division. Let no group or individual within the church have an eye for its own interests alone, but also for the rest. May God save us from being so exclusively occupied with our own interests that we are completely unconscious of others; for when we yield to selfishness, we lose in the end. Our Lord said: "Whosoever shall seek to save his life shall lose it; and whosoever shall lose his life shall preserve it" (Luke 17:33). If we look out for the interests of others, God will look out for us.

Later in the same chapter in Philippians Paul sounds a sad note when he says:

> For all seek their own, not the things which are Jesus Christ's.
>
> Phil. 2:21

My interests must be bound up in the spiritual welfare of my brethren in Christ. There is too much of the spirit of Cain among us. It impudently asks, "Am I my brother's keeper?" (Gen. 4:9) Cain yielded to the dictates of a selfish heart. We cannot afford to do so. For the believer there is no road that bypasses a brother in Christ. May it please our Heavenly Father to arouse the carnal, pleasure-bent, self-indulgent professing Christian in many of our churches to a new interest in the needs of others.

IX. PATTERN

Let this mind be in you, which was also in Christ Jesus:
Who, being in the form of God, thought it not robbery to be equal with God:
But made Himself of no reputation, and took upon Him the form of a servant, and was made in the likeness of man:
And being found in fashion as a man, He humbled Himself, and became obedient unto death, even the death of the cross.
Wherefore God also hath highly exalted Him, and given Him a name which is above every name:
That at the name of Jesus every knee should bow, of things in heaven, and things in earth, and things under the earth;
And that every tongue should confess that Jesus Christ is Lord, to the glory of God the Father.

Philippians 2:5-11

These seven verses of Scripture form one of the most sublime and majestic paragraphs on the Person of Jesus Christ to be found anywhere. This passage, in its scriptural setting and context, provides the perfect pattern for humility. The inspired writer has been pleading for lowliness, and now he moves from the *Plea* to the *Pattern*. Of course, Christ is that Pattern. Every divinely-ordered virtue enjoined upon God's children is exhibited in the Man, Christ Jesus our Lord. So Paul points the saints to the Saviour. He says:

Let this mind be in you, which was also in Christ Jesus.

Phil. 2:5

This verse is not an appeal to the believer to strive for the intellectual perfection that was Christ's. As a man, He was, what no other man ever can be, God. His was the omniscient mind of deity. However, we are asked to have in us the same moral attitude which was in Christ, for His human life on earth was the highest example of self-forgetfulness and deep concern for others. We must contemplate in ourselves the spirit of humility and self-abnegation that our Lord so richly demonstrated. Seemingly this grace was lacking among the Philippian Christians; hence their spiritual need gave rise to one of the most profound Christological arguments ever written. Our Lord is here set forth as a lowly Servant whose attitude and actions should be cherished by all the redeemed. Complete resignation to the Father's will and service to others characterized His entire life on earth. "Let this mind be in you." Don't think selfishly about your own interests, but live for God and others.

Guided by the Holy Spirit, the apostle shows us the two extremes of our Saviour's majesty and humility. He points one finger to the sovereign throne of deity and the other to the shameful cross of death, and he shows us, step by step, the greatest demonstrations of voluntary servitude and sacrifice man or God has ever witnessed. This pen picture of our Lord's descent from sovereignty to shame is here set forth that it might inspire us, not to be taken up with ourselves and our interests, but to be willing to stoop, if need be, to the lowest depths for the glory of God and the good of others. The mind of Christ is the attitude of humility that leads to crucifixion. We see Him as He was and is in the following verses.

A. *The Sovereign*

Who, being in the form of God, thought it not robbery to be equal with God.

Phil. 2:6

Here is a statement of the fact of Christ's deity. Was He God or was He merely like God? Before His Incarnation in Bethlehem He existed "in the form of God." Deity always was a part of His very "being." He did not become God when He became man. His deity predated His human experience on earth. His deity predated Bethlehem and Mary. "In the *beginning*" He "was with God, and . . . was God" (John 1:1). In His Incarnation He was "God manifest in the flesh" (1 Tim. 3:16). Before ever our Lord stooped to identify Himself with the human race, He was one with the Father. To those who questioned His deity, He said: "Before Abraham was, I am" (John 8:58).

He was in "the form of God" before He took upon Him "the form of a servant." The word "form" does not apply to outward appearances and characteristics, but rather to the very essence and nature of "God" in verse 6, and the very essence and nature of a true "servant" in verse 7. What He looked like in outward appearance is described as "fashion" in verse 8. The "form" indicates what He was; the "fashion," what He looked like.

A certain ladies' garment manufacturer requires its models to be a specified weight and height. These young women are the forms, while the garments they wear are the fashion.

Our Lord Jesus Christ was in the form of God, that

is, God is what He was. In His Incarnation He put on "fashion as a man" and "was made in the likeness of men." The point in verse 6 is that Jesus Christ is co-eternal, coessential, and coequal with the Father. So emphatic was our Lord in teaching His essential deity that those who heard Him sought to kill Him because He was "making Himself equal with God" (John 5:18).

The apostle here adds that Christ "thought it not robbery to be equal with God."

What is meant by this statement? Our present usage of the word "robbery" will convey the meaning. When we hear of a robbery we think at once of someone unlawfully taking something that was another's. Now our Lord claimed deity. He said: "I and My Father are one . . . he that hath seen Me hath seen the Father" (John 10:30; 14:9).

Was He truly God or did He falsely seize upon a title not rightfully His? He did not regard His claims of equality with the Father as something pilfered. What He claimed was His by inherent and eternal right. Many false Christs have laid claims to deity, but our Lord Jesus was truly God, and the physical manifestation He assumed in His Incarnation was the "fashion" whereby God could be perceived by man. When He said He was coequal and coeternal with the Father, He told the truth and did not grasp after something that was not truly His. John said: "And the Word was made flesh, and dwelt among us, (and we beheld His glory, the glory as of the only begotten of the Father,) full of grace and truth. . . . No man hath seen God at any time; the only begotten Son, which is in the bosom of the Father,

He hath declared Him" (John 1:14, 18). Others might have cheated in their endeavor to lay hold of a costly and coveted prize, but never the Holy One.

B. *The Servant*

But made Himself of no reputation, and took upon Him the form of a servant, and was made in the likeness of men.
Phil. 2:7

Even though He was God He did not insist upon being served, but laid aside temporarily the full and final exercise of the Sovereign and became the Servant.

The phrase "made Himself of no reputation" has been translated, "He emptied Himself." Theologians have referred to this as "the Kenosis," or "the self-emptying." In His Incarnation and Crucifixion, Christ divested Himself of something. But of what? Certainly He did not empty Himself of His deity, for that could never be. He fused manhood and deity into a union, but in so doing He did not, nay, He could not, cease to be God.

We must face the fact that our verse does not tell us of what Christ emptied Himself. J. C. Muller says: "The Kenosis (emptying) of Christ existed in His 'taking the form of a servant' and 'being made in the likeness of men.' " There is no mention of His abandoning any of the essential attributes of deity. At His Incarnation He did not lay aside "the form of God," but He merely took something to Himself: namely, "the form of a servant." When He enrobed Himself in flesh and enslaved Himself for humanity, He laid aside certain rights as God the eternal Son, but of His deity, never!

Keep in mind that Paul has been pleading for low-liness of mind, humility of spirit, among believers. How perfectly and completely our Lord demonstrated genuine humility! In His infinite stoop from sovereignty to slavery, God became a man, and just as He possessed the full essence of deity, He "was made in the likeness of men," taking upon Him the very essence of humanity, apart from sin. In His self-abnegation He identified Himself with us in His humiliation. He took upon Him a body like ours and faced a limited human existence on earth. The world has never witnessed a truer expression of self-renunciation. When we ponder the fact that God became Man, labored with His hands, faced life in every respect as Man, served, sorrowed, and suffered, we stand in holy awe and wonder at so great condescension. The Sovereign of all became the Servant of all.

Let each of us learn one of life's greatest lessons from our divine Saviour and Lord. We throw our weight around to impress others. We assume a role we actually are not. We struggle for a reputation. He *"made Himself of no reputation."* He stooped. He stepped down. Behold Him, and then *"let each esteem other better than themselves."*

The Sovereign became the Servant, the Bondslave, but Bondslave to whom? One says: "To the whole race of mankind." This is true as far as it goes, but it stops short of a complete and satisfying answer. He was first, foremost, and finally the Servant of the Father. "Behold, My servant" (Isaiah 52:13)! Yes, He served us all and He served well, but in the steps down to the role of Servant, He said: "I come . . . to do Thy will, O God" (Heb. 10:7). Let this mind be in you.

C. *The Sacrifice*

And being found in fashion as a man, He humbled Himself, and became obedient unto death, even the death of the cross.

Phil. 2:8

Each step down brought Him into deeper humiliation and finally death. From glory to Golgotha He trod a path of humiliation which culminated in a voluntary, vicarious sacrifice for sinful mankind. Dying for sin He need not have died, because He was sinless, and death was the penalty for sin. But this He chose that He might become our Substitute and Saviour. There were other forms of death from which He might have selected, but He chose to go as low as one could go by submitting to the most degrading and shameful, the most painful and ignominious form of death known to man, *"even the death of the cross."*

Beware here of misunderstanding when the text says He "became obedient *unto* death." It does not mean that He surrendered to become subservient to death. He is, and ever will be, the mighty Victor over death. He proved this when He arose from the grave in triumph over death. One of the purposes of His Incarnation was to defeat, and ultimately destroy, the angel of death. "Forasmuch then as the children are partakers of flesh and blood, He also Himself likewise took part of the same; that through death He might destroy him that had the power of death, that is, the devil; And deliver them who through fear of death were all their lifetime subject to bondage" (Heb. 2:14-15). After His ascension

He testified: "I am He that liveth, and was dead; and, behold, I am alive for evermore, Amen; and have the keys of hell and of death" (Rev. 1:18).

Death marked the ultimate point of obedience, the extent to which He went. And then He chose a form of death reserved for slaves and criminals. By his sacrifice He displayed humility and obedience to an extent that no other ever could display it. History has no parallel. As one contemplates in solemn silence such holy condescension of deity in the dust, one must fall at the feet of the crucified One and confess the wonder of His glorious love and man's own worthlessness. It was a long way down from Heaven's throne to Calvary's cross. Do we catch a glimpse of what true humility is? Let this mind be in you.

D. *The Sovereign Again*

Wherefore God also hath highly exalted Him, and given Him a name which is above every name:

That at the name of Jesus every knee should bow, of things in heaven, and things in earth, and things under the earth;

And that every tongue should confess that Jesus Christ is Lord, to the glory of God the Father.

Phil. 2:9-11

Rather striking is the fact that the One who humbled Himself is once more exalted, and here His exaltation is extended to a larger sphere than before. At no time since Christ's first Advent has "every knee" bowed to Him and "every tongue" confessed His Lordship. But because of His voluntary act of humility and self-renunciation, He is to be exalted to the highest rank and authority, to supreme sovereignty.

At His first coming in humiliation He was given a name. "And she shall bring forth a son, and thou shalt call His name JESUS: for He shall save His people from their sins" (Matt. 1:21).

Only a small per cent of the human race has respected and revered that Name. In public the Name of Jesus Christ is heard more often in cursing and blasphemy than in reverence and respect. To Christians that Name is as precious ointment poured forth. It is in His Name that remission of sins is preached among all nations (Luke 24:47). It is in His Name that God's children come to Him in prayer (John 16:23). True believers who love God's dear Son gladly own His Name in all places. But that Name is despised by many.

A day is coming, and some of us believe it is not too far away, when God's exalted Son will come to earth the second time, and every creature will be in subjection to the mighty Sovereign. In that day the earth will be filled with the glory of the Lord. Everywhere, among all nations and races of men, knees will bow and tongues will confess that Jesus Christ is Lord to the Glory of God the Father. In our day multitudes kneel to Roman popes, but in that day all popes and their followers, all Jews, all Gentiles will be forced to bow and confess before Him whom they have humiliated and dishonored. This scene that Paul depicts is not the error of a final restoration of all souls, as some teach. Paul's words do not point to a willing worship of the Lord Jesus Christ. Such a view has no support in Scripture. Christ's subjects in that day will be no more willing to worship Him than are the masses of men today.

There is a spiritual truth stated clearly in the Bible

which says: "For whosoever exalteth himself shall be abased; and he that humbleth himself shall be exalted" (Luke 14:11).

Christ concerned Himself with humility. The Father did the exalting. It is this lesson in our Philippian passage the Spirit of God would impress upon our hearts. Christ's mind must be in us. His mental and moral attitude toward others must be ours. We must be willing to take the form of servants, to be rebuked, misunderstood, even despised. If we are not willing to suffer with Him, and for Him now, we cannot reign with Him then (2 Tim. 2:12). "Humble yourselves therefore under the mighty hand of God, that He may exalt you in due time" (1 Peter 5:6).

X. PROCESS

Wherefore, my beloved, as you have always obeyed, not as in my presence only, but now much more in my absence, work out your own salvation with fear and trembling,

For it is God which worketh in you both to will and to do of His good pleasure.

Do all things without murmurings and disputings:

That ye may be blameless and harmless, the sons of God, without rebuke, in the midst of a crooked and perverse nation, among whom ye shine as lights in the world;

Holding forth the word of life; that I may rejoice in the day of Christ, that I have not run in vain, neither laboured in vain.

Yea, and if I be offered upon the sacrifice and service of your faith, I joy, and rejoice with you all.

For the same cause also do ye joy, and rejoice with me.

Philippians 2:12-18

Thus far in the second chapter of this Epistle, the apostle has set forth the *Plea* and the *Pattern*. The *Plea* is for self-renunciation, for lowliness of mind, and humility. Then the sublime example of Christ is set before us as the perfect *Pattern*. In this section Paul presents a *process* whereby attainment is possible.

In the process there is something to learn. The Christian must cultivate the good practice of standing on his own feet and not depending solely on others. As in 1:27, here again Paul reminds his readers that they cannot go on depending upon him. Whatever obedience they rendered to God when Paul was yet with them will not carry them along to spiritual maturity during his absence.

The work of salvation was begun in his presence when he was in Philippi; however, he writes, "but now much more in my absence, work out your own salvation with fear and trembling."

The apostle's statement, telling the saints to work out their own salvation, has been a perplexing one to many who have been taught that salvation, from start to finish, is dependent upon God's grace. Now we know that redemption is all of grace, "For by grace are ye saved through faith; and that not of yourselves; it is the gift of God: Not of works, lest any man should boast" (Eph. 2:8-9).

But we see how these verses are followed immediately by Christian responsibility. Paul adds: "For we are His workmanship, created in Christ Jesus unto good works, which God hath before ordained that we should walk in them" (Eph. 2:10).

The saved man is God's workmanship, but he is also a workman himself. His obedience to truth (his good works) should not depend upon his nearness to spiritual oversight and Christian influence. Victorious Christian living, in obedience to the truths of God's Word, never relaxes. Some professing believers have an outward show of obedience when they are within sight and sound of of godly persons, but let them be found in a place where they are unwatched, and one might question if ever they possessed a salvation to work out. God nowhere is said to call upon an unsaved person to work out a salvation that He has not worked in, but He fully expects the inwrought work of regeneration to be worked out by the regenerated one.

Writing to those who were already saved, Paul admonished them, whether they faced an assembly problem or a personal problem, to work it out to its ultimate and victorious conclusion as one might work out a mathematical problem to its final and correct answer.

Salvation in Scripture is a mighty subject including practical sanctification as well as judicial justification. Only God can declare a man judicially righteous, but once He does this, then the one who is righteous positionally is expected to make progress practically. The Philippian saints had started well and were walking the path of obedience when Paul departed from them, but they were to continue on in that same pathway. Paul had been instructing them. Now they were on their own. They must look to Jesus Christ, treading the path that He trod, even if it led them to surrender everything and left them with only the Cross. Such a course would be a lonely and difficult one, but there was to be no let up in their working at it.

"Work out your own salvation." When I visited the West Indies in 1956, I witnessed American aluminum manufacturers removing millions of tons of bauxite from the hills of Jamaica. The rich ore was already there. God had worked it in by some catastrophic movement of nature or through some aging process. Man had only to operate and exploit in order to get the greatest worth out of that which already was his possession. As I watched I observed the process to be anything but simple and easy. It was a costly project. But be certain, the effort was sure to pay off in large dividends. Such, it seems to me, is the idea in the Holy Spirit's words, "work out your own salvation." It is my possession by the gift of divine grace, but as Guy H. King has said:

"I am to mine what is already mine," endeavoring to work out that precious nugget of humility.

And then Paul adds, "with fear and trembling." Here is a pertinent point in the process, not to be overlooked. The words "fear and trembling" occur in several places in Paul's writings. He testified how he ministered the word in fear and trembling (1 Cor. 2:3), and how they received Titus with fear and trembling (2 Cor. 7:15), and that servants were to obey their masters with fear and trembling (Eph. 6:5). Now here in Philippians he is telling them to work out their own salvation with fear and trembling, not fear and trembling lest they lose their salvation, for no truly saved person will be lost, but because of the weakness of the flesh, the ways of the world, and the wiles of the devil.

We need to fear the flesh since it is weak and will fail us every time. We need to fear the world because it is ready to let loose its criticism at our failures. We need to fear Satan because he is ever seeking to break down our resistance that we might fall into temptation. We can do with some of this reverential fear and holy trembling before God to serve as a bulwark against trusting in ourselves and the temptation to do wrong. Working out our own salvation in fear and trembling is taking heed lest we fall (1 Cor. 10:12). In other words, do not trust in yourself, and never feel that you have done your best to meet God's righteous standard. This verse is teaching human responsibility.

In the next verse we have the divine enablement:

For it is God which worketh in you both to will and to do of His good pleasure.

Phil. 2:13

Here the word "worketh" means "to energize." The saints are to continue working out their salvation realizing that this can be accomplished only as we do so in fellowship with God. He only can energize us for this daily task, for He is putting forth His power in us. In an earlier Epistle, Paul testified: "For He that wrought effectually in Peter to the apostleship of the circumcision, the same was mighty in me toward the Gentiles" (Gal. 2:8).

He who worked mightily in Paul "worketh in you." It is not merely that He *has* worked, or that He *will* work, but that He works *now*. At any moment in our Christian experience we may draw from the unlimited Source of divine power. "Now unto Him that is able to do exceeding abundantly above all that we ask or think, according to the power that worketh in us" (Eph. 3:20).

We work and God works. It is a mutual effort toward the common goal of glorifying God in our lives. Here is a blending and interacting of God's sovereign grace and power and man's free will. God works in us but we dare not be passive. We work, too, and our work and the exercise of our wills are never at greater liberty than when thus engaged in doing "His good pleasure." The Holy Spirit abides in the believer, and He is never more pleased than when we are working out that which He has worked in. God and the Christian make up a team that all the forces of evil cannot overthrow. But remember, while God has assumed the responsibility for the inworking, we are responsible for the outworking.

If God has begun His good work in you, then carry it on, as you surely may with His help. There is no soundness in the philosophy of fatalism that says, "What is to be, will be," whether we co-work with God or not. The power and ability are of God, but it belongs to us to surrender to His will in complete obedience. Some may call this a paradox. But what of it? I know that God's sovereignty is a fact, and I know, from personal experience as well as from the clear statements of Scripture, that man's human responsibility is a fact. Do we not have the same principle stated elsewhere by Paul, where he says: "I have planted, Apollos watered; but God gave the increase" (1 Cor. 3:6).

God is working in you now! Will you begin to work it out? Let me share with you a paragraph from the pen of the late F. B. Meyer: "He may be working in you to confess to that fellow-Christian that you were unkind in your speech or act. Work it out. He may be working in you to give up that line of business about which you have been doubtful lately. Give it up. He may be working in you to be sweeter in your home, and gentler in your speech. Begin. He may be working in you to alter your relations with some with whom you have dealings that are not as they should be. Alter them. This very day let God begin to speak, and work and will; and then work out what He works in. God will not work apart from you, but He wants to work through you. Let Him. Yield to Him, and let this be the day when you shall begin to live in the power of the mighty Indwelling One."

So divine sovereignty and human responsibility meet at the crossroads of some mighty decisions. And remember, the sign marked "His good pleasure" is the only one worth following.

In working out their salvation as it related to assembly problems, the Philippians were exhorted as follows:

Do all things without murmurings and disputings:

That ye may be blameless and harmless, the sons of God, without rebuke, in the midst of a crooked and perverse nation, among whom ye shine as lights in the world.

Phil. 2:14-15

Here is some much needed advice for the "children of God." Christians must face their problems "without murmurings," that is, without half-concealed, half-uttered complaints, as F. A. Noble so aptly puts it. Murmuring Christians are seldom of any use in the cause of Christ. If only God's children would stop their whisperings about this one or that one, about this policy or that policy. Beware of the grumbling undertone! Do not join the devil's crowd by engaging your energies in stirring up strife. When referring to the murmurings of the children of Israel as recorded by Moses in Numbers 20:2 and 21:5, Paul writes: "Neither murmur ye, as some of them also murmured, and were destroyed of the destroyer" (1 Cor. 10:10).

Murmurings, if allowed to continue, will result in "disputings." We must check all such disrupting and dividing influences, whether in our own lives or in the lives of others, the very first time they rear their insidious heads. Were God to remove the disgruntled church members from some of our local churches, few would be left to do God's work. It is so unlike Christ to find fault with, and criticize, that which is being done for God. Our work for the Lord in the local assembly calls for the saints to band together before Him, and deal with each problem in the light of His Word. Murmurings and disputings break our fellowship with God and with one another. Casting out these two ugly monsters is a part of the divine process for making the believer like Christ. Oh, my brethren, let us pray God to rid us of all inward discontent.

By working out our own salvation we arrive at a goal in this present life. That goal is the bringing of the unsaved out of darkness into light. By our lives others see us as God would have us:

> . . . blameless and harmless, the sons of God, without rebuke, in the midst of a crooked and perverse nation, among whom ye shine as lights in the world.
>
> Phil. 2:15

"Blameless," as used here, means to be without fault before others. Before our fellow-Christians and the unsaved we must carry ourselves beyond reproach. Certainly I am not working out my salvation if my life has in it that which is inconsistent with my high calling in Christ. I am sure the enemies of God looked for some fault in Daniel when they sought to find occasion against him, but we read: "Then the presidents and princes sought to find occasion against Daniel concerning the kingdom; but they could find none occasion nor fault; forasmuch as he was faithful, neither was there any error or fault found in him" (Dan. 6:4).

When the test came, Daniel patiently worked out his salvation thereby leaving a good testimony in the midst of a crooked and perverse nation. He was shining as a light in the world of his day. Thus we, in our generation, must seek to do likewise amidst the spiritual darkness about us. We have failed when we cause others to stumble.

"Harmless" has to do more with our inward state. Our

thoughts and motives are to be guileless, unmixed with selfishness and insincerity, unadulterated. The end to which God is working in His children is to effect fruit both outwardly and inwardly. And let not one of us ever underestimate the importance of inward correctness, because no mere outward show of right living can long be maintained when the heart is not right in God's sight. Guard well the inner man. Keep the secret chambers of the heart pure.

It is our Heavenly Father's desire that we be *"sons of God, without rebuke."* All true believers in Christ are the sons of God now, and neither time nor growth in grace can make us more the sons of God than we are now. The goal is that we become sons of God *"without rebuke."* The words "without rebuke" have in them the idea of being "without blemish," or "without defect." This goal will be reached when our blessed Lord comes in the air to gather His Church to Himself. At that time He will "present it to Himself a glorious church, not having spot, or wrinkle, or any such thing; but that it should be holy and without blemish" (Eph. 5:27). But while we wait for His Coming, we have a mission for God. Paul adds: "Shine as lights in the world" (Phil. 2:15).

Christ has put His Church in the world to shine as lights, but too frequently has the world eaten its way into the Church and dimmed the light. As the sons of God we are Heaven's royal representatives "in the midst of a crooked and perverse nation." The world is twisted morally and spiritually, following its own pattern while it refuses to recognize God's plan. Men evade the truth to follow their own definite reasoning. In this kind of world, God calls upon His children to reflect the Light of the world, our Lord and Saviour Jesus Christ.

How are we to do this? The answer follows clearly:

> Holding forth the word of life; that I may rejoice in the day of Christ, that I have not run in vain, neither laboured in vain.
>
> Phil. 2:16

Here is something every Christian can and should do. We can hold forth the gift of God's Word to those in darkness. In this we may neither hold out nor hold back. Our resources must be combined in an all-out effort to proclaim the gospel. It is a poor testimony indeed to put into God's service what little remains of our time, strength, and money, after we have spent most of it to satisfy our own selfish desires.

Paul did not live to please himself. He lived and labored in the light of *"the day of Christ."* In that day he wanted to rejoice in abiding fruit. So he held forth the Word of life. To waste his time in performing works that have no lasting spiritual qualities, and that would be burned up, would be to labor in vain. He who would shine as a light must burn. No candle can give light without the wax being consumed. No lamp can give light if its oil is not being consumed. John the Baptist was "a burning and a shining light" (John 5:35). So was Paul!

> Yea, and if I be offered upon the sacrifice and service of your faith, I joy, and rejoice with you all.
>
> For the same cause also do ye joy, and rejoice with me.
>
> Phil. 2:17, 18

The apostle's life in Christ was one continuous sacrifice. He suffered much in order that he might take God's Word to those in darkness. And now, if the divine process demands that he give his life, he is ready to die as his last full measure of devotion and sacrifice in behalf of Christ. The divine process for his Lord was good enough for Paul. To be poured out in death gives him no hard nor heavy heart, but only joy and rejoicing.

"I joy . . . rejoice with me." He has caught the spirit of the Lord Jesus, "who for the joy that was set before Him endured the cross" (Heb. 12:2). No less than eighteen times Paul uses the words "joy," "rejoice," or "rejoicing" in the Philippian letter. This is the keynote of the entire Epistle. It is the "joy way," the path of sacrificial service. Our Lord walked this way. So did Paul. So may you and I.

XI. PARTNERS

But I trust in the Lord Jesus to send Timotheus shortly unto you, that I also may be of good comfort, when I know your state.

For I have no man likeminded, who will naturally care for your state.

For all seek their own, not the things which are Jesus Christ's.

But ye know the proof of him, that, as a son with the father, he hath served with me in the gospel.

Him therefore I hope to send presently, so soon as I shall see how it will go with me.

But I trust in the Lord that I also myself shall come shortly.

Yet I supposed it necessary to send to you Epaphroditus, my brother, and companion in labour, and fellowsoldier, but your messenger, and he that ministered to my wants.

For he longed after you all, and was full of heaviness, because that ye had heard that he had been sick.

For indeed he was sick nigh unto death: but God had mercy on him; and not on him only, but on me also, lest I should have sorrow upon sorrow.

I sent him therefore the more carefully, that, when ye see him again, ye may rejoice, and that I may be the less sorrowful.

Receive him therefore in the Lord with all gladness; and hold such in reputation:

Because for the work of Christ, he was nigh unto death, not regarding his life, to supply your lack of service toward me.

Philippians 2:19-30

We are about to be introduced to two worthy men of God, fine examples of all that Paul has been teaching us in this second chapter. We have just been learning about *"lowliness"* (2:3) and about *"lights"* (2:15); and now we have in two of Paul's partners magnificient examples of both. Timothy and Epaphroditus are here set before us as witnesses to the possibility of self-renounced and sacrificial living.

Three thoughts shall engage our attention in the twelve verses before us.

A. *Pastoral Concern*

Throughout the Epistle Paul has shown a genuine interest in and a deep concern for the saints at Philippi. He never ceased to thank God for them and to pray in their behalf. Twice in close succession he uses the term "your state" (2:19, 20). His great pastoral heart could not allow him to grow lax in manifesting concern for them. Having been present when some of them received their spiritual birth, his whole life remained bound up in theirs. He wanted to know their condition and to help where needed. In his own words he expresses his desire, to "know your state" and to "care for your state."

Before Paul's mind is the stark fact of the uncertainty of life (2:17). His sufferings for the cause of Christ had been so intense, he sees before him the possibility of death in the immediate future. And now, as he thinks of this coming sacrifice, his greatest desire is to be of further service to saints and to sinners in Christ's Name. To serve his Lord to the end is the bright project set before him. One of the last things Paul wrote was his stirring and touching testimony as follows: "For I am now ready to be offered, and the time of my departure is at hand. I have fought a good fight, I have finished my course, I have kept the faith: Henceforth there is laid up for me a crown of righteousness, which the Lord, the righteous judge, shall give me at that day: and not to me only, but unto all them also that love His appearing" (2 Tim. 4:6-8).

From the day Christ saved Paul on the Damascus thruway, his life was lived in sacrificial service for others. His charge to the elders of Ephesus was no empty boast when he said: "But none of these things move me, neither count I my life dear unto myself, so that I might finish my course with joy, and the ministry, which I have received of the Lord Jesus, to testify the gospel of the grace of God" (Acts 20:24).

Here is pastoral concern at its truest and highest. Here is a clear instance of unselfishness. Here is devotedness and lowliness at its best. How like the Great Shepherd of the sheep was the Apostle! Paul followed closely in the steps of his great Leader whose life of service and sacrifice for others led Him to the Cross. Paul stood out in his day as a shepherd of souls.

Our times need more ministers like him who will look out for the souls of others. May God give to His Church holy men who care nothing for personal gain and comfort but who are willing to follow the path of sacrifice for the achievement of its divinely-chosen goals. The mind of Christ is the model for the mind of the minister. The passion of Christ is the pattern for every pastor.

B. *Pathetic Conditions*

For all seek their own, not the things which are Jesus Christ's.

Phil. 2.21

This is in contrast to Paul's *pastoral concern* for his brethren. This pathetic condition of self-seeking is the curse of Christendom in general and of the ministry in particular. Paul's words are a scathing indictment against the awful sin of selfishness. It must have been present in the early Church, for we remember his exhortation at the beginning of our chapter: "Look not every man on his own things, but every man also on the things of others" (2:4).

There are so few who devote their lives in selfless service. We are more concerned with *our* interests, *our* goods, *our* getting ahead, than we are with the needs of others. Genuine Christian love "seeketh not her own" (1 Cor. 13:5). "Let no man, then, set his own advantage as his objective, but rather the good of his neighbor (1 Cor. 10:24, Phillips).

In spite of these holy admonitions, self-seeking and self-glorifying gain momentum with the passing of time. Few are seeking to follow closely in the steps of Christ and of Christlike men such as Paul. Most of us seek our own interests while we profess Christ's Name. One wonders if the claims of Christ ever enter the calculations of some Christians. The late William Lincoln of Beresford, London, said: "Rest assured, that if you put Christ in the second place, and your own things in the first, you will hear of it at the Judgment Seat."

I am reminded of the too frequent occasions when I have been unwilling to surrender my comfort and my concern for my things for the holy cause of my Lord, I must recall it to my shame. I read of Demas who forsook God's suffering, dying servant because he loved this present world (2 Tim. 4:10), and of Diotrephes who loved "to have the preeminence" among the brethren (3 John 9); but I must hold my critical fire. These men did what I, and some of you, have done. One difference is that we have had nineteen centuries of Christianity behind us from which we should have profited. These centuries have made available to us the Holy Scriptures, much of which those men never saw. I doubt that the losses of Demas and Diotrephes will be as great as ours.

Guy H. King writes that: "When Sir Bartle Frere returned from India the carriage was sent to the village station to bring him to his home. When the new footman, but newly engaged, asked how he should recognize Sir Bartle, his aged mother said, 'Look out for somebody helping someone else.' Sure enough, when the London train had drawn in, the manservant observed a gentle-man assisting an old lady to the platform and then jumping back into the carriage to fetch out her luggage. Going straight up to him, the footman enquired, 'Sir Bartle?' Yes; it was he. What a lovely reputation to have! To be known as one who is always on the lookout to see when, and how, one can help others."

Do I seem to exaggerate when I tell you that the pathetic conditions in Paul's day are magnified in ours? Is it not pathetically true that the percentage of Christians who are willing to forego their own comfort and advantage, for the things of Jesus Christ, is all too small? Imagine what blessing would come to our hearts, homes, churches, and communities, were we to put the cause of Christ in the foreground with self-forgetful, sacrificial devotion! Paul's readiness to obey his Lord stands in sharp contrast to the rest of us. Is your heart, and mine, ready now to lay aside any special interest and endeavor in order that we might serve Christ more acceptably?

C. *Profitable Companions*

These were Paul's partners in serving Christ. Timotheus and Epaphroditus were willing co-workers in the gospel with Paul. They were men on whom the apostle could depend; ready to be sent anywhere, ready to serve anyone, and ready to sacrifice anything.

They were ready to be sent anywhere. "I trust in the Lord Jesus to send Timotheus shortly unto you" (2:19), and "I supposed it necessary to send to you Epaphroditus" (2:25), says Paul. The apostle's words "to send Timotheus" and "to send Epaphroditus" gave cause for rejoicing, not because of Paul's decision to send them, but because of their dedication to go. Like Isaiah of old, they were ready to go wherever God would send them. "Also I heard the voice of the Lord, saying, Whom shall I send, and who will go for us? Then said I, Here am I, send me" (Isaiah 6:8).

God is calling young men to go! "And He said unto them, Go ye into all the world, and preach the gospel to every creature" (Mark 16:15).

Christians are Christ's "sent ones" to the untold and the untaught. The key word of the New Testament to the believer is "go." To the maniac of Gadara, whom Christ saved, He said: "Go home to thy friends, and tell them how great things the Lord hath done for thee, and hath had compassion on thee" (Mark 5:19).

The Lord is not sending some of us far from home to some pagan part of the world, but nevertheless He is sending us to those who are nearest to us. He is sending us to our loved ones and friends. Praise God for faithful Andrew. John says: "He first findeth his own brother Simon, and saith unto him. We have found the Messias, which is, being interpreted, the Christ. And he brought him to Jesus" (John 1:41-42).

Andrew did not go far, just far enough to win his brother to Christ, who, in turn, saw three thousand souls converted when he preached his first sermon. Somehow I feel that Andrew will be rewarded for three thousand and one, the fruit of the Pentecostal sermon plus Peter. It pays to go where God sends. Timotheus and Epaphroditus were ready to be sent anywhere. Suppose God made it clear to you that He wanted you to go somewhere to minister to someone; would you go? Jesus said: "A certain man had two sons; and he came to the first, and said, Son, go work to day in my vineyard. He answered and said, I will not: but afterward he repented, and went. And he came to the second, and said likewise. And he answered and said, I go, sir: and went not" (Matt. 21: 28-30).

Some of you are like the son who said he would go but who went not. Others can be compared to the son who refused to go when sent. Whatever your case may be, repent of your disobedience at once, and say with Isaiah, "Here am I, send me." Timotheus and Epaphroditus were ready to be sent anywhere. Are you?

They were ready to serve anyone. Paul testified of Timotheus:

> But yet know the proof of him, that, as a son with the father, he hath served with me in the gospel.
>
> Phil. 2:22

The Apostle wrote also of Epaphroditus:

My . . . companion in labour . . . your messenger, and he that ministered to my wants.

Phil. 2:25

Timothy "will naturally care for your state," Paul tells them in verse 20. There is nobody like him who will look after and attend to the interests of others. He is a tried and tested servant of the Lord. Paul's own testimony bears witness to this fact in verse 22. Timothy, like Paul, had the mind of Christ in his devoted service to others.

Man is basically selfish by nature, but when he becomes completely yielded to Jesus Christ, he is, like his Lord, no respecter of persons. Jesus testified: "The Spirit of the Lord is upon Me, because He hath anointed Me to preach the gospel to the poor; He hath sent Me to heal the brokenhearted, to preach deliverance to the captives, and recovering of sight to the blind, to set at liberty them that are bruised" (Luke 4:18).

If only we would sit longer at Jesus' feet and learn of Him, we would imbibe some of the selflessness of the greatest Servant of all. A man who takes Christ's yoke upon him will never refuse to serve anyone. Timothy, like Paul, was a great soul. He was "like-souled" (verse 20) (a translation of "likeminded") *naturally*. The word "naturally" has in it the idea of *"genuinely, sincerely."* There was nothing spurious about Timothy's willingness to serve anyone. He was not as those hypocrites whom our Lord condemned for doing good things for others to gain a reputation for themselves (Matt. 6:1-2). Thus Timothy could be depended upon to manifest a genuine interest in others.

They were ready to sacrifice anything. There is little else, if anything, in Scripture about Epaphroditus, apart from that which Paul gives to us here. If we had known nothing else about him, there is sufficient in these verses to give us a picture of his heart. He hazarded his life for others. Twice Paul reminds his readers that Epaphroditus was "nigh unto death" (verses 27, 30). He is described here by various names. He is Paul's "brother," "companion in labour," "fellowsoldier," and "your messenger."

Epaphroditus was the "messenger" who brought the church's gift from Philippi to Paul at Rome. The journey was doubtless a difficult one, for Epaphroditus became ill. Paul writes:

> For indeed he was sick nigh unto death: but God had mercy on him; and not on him only, but on me also, lest I should have sorrow upon sorrow.
>
> Phil. 2:27

And now that all may rejoice in God's miracle-working power in behalf of Epaphroditus, Paul plans to send him back to Philippi. When the saints there knew he had arrived safely among them, they would have no further cause for anxiety.

I think that Paul's descriptive term, "fellowsoldier," just about explains the man Epaphroditus. He recklessly staked everything by flinging himself into the fray against the powers of darkness. He endured hardness as a good soldier of Jesus Christ (2 Tim. 2:3). In the conflict for Christ he was brought to the very door of death, but he never counted the cost. Good soldiers never do. They are ready to sacrifice anything, even their lives if necessary.

Christianity is worth living for and worth dying for. Any Christian who goes all-out in soldiering for Jesus Christ will embark on the greatest adventure possible. And though one might sacrifice his life in the battle, he has gained in the end. Jesus says: "For whosoever will save his life shall lose it: but whosoever will lose his life for my sake, the same shall save it" (Luke 9:24).

Where is the man in our generation who, like Paul and Barnabas (Acts 15:26) and Epaphroditus (Phil. 2:30), is "not regarding his life"? God help each of us to be willing to sacrifice anything. If we continue to live selfishly, life may be prolonged on earth, but not for God's glory and our eternal good. How sweet the fragrance of the lives of Paul and his partners! And how rebuked does this writer feel!

XII. PRECAUTION

Finally, my brethren, rejoice in the Lord. To write the same things to you, to me indeed is not grievous, but for you it is safe.

Beware of dogs, beware of evil workers, beware of the concision.

For we are the circumcision, which worship God in the spirit, and rejoice in Christ Jesus, and have no confidence in the flesh.

Philippians 3:1-3

The "finally" used here does not mean that Paul is about to conclude his letter. I am satisfied that he has not used the word carelessly, as do some preachers. Wuest translates the word "finally" to read "as for the rest." Paul uses it again in Philippians 4:8. It appears that the apostle jubilantly is saying, "As for the rest, my brethren, nothing remains but to rejoice in the Lord." This brings us to the first of three precautionary thoughts given to serve as a protective for the children of God. We might call these the three protectives. First, rejoice in the Lord. Secondly, resist the enemy. Thirdly, refrain from the flesh.

A. *Rejoice in the Lord*

Here again Paul strikes the note of joy which is the keynote of the Epistle. He speaks of this blessed characteristic, in some form, no less than eighteen times. He was conscious, no doubt, of the repetition; for he says: "To write the same things to you, to me indeed is not grievous, but for you it is safe." Reiteration was never irksome to Paul because it is one of the basic principles for effective teaching. To repeat the message of joy was not tiring or tedious for him; and as for the rest of the saints, no harm or hardship could come to them because of it. Anything worth saying once is worth repeating. Who of us does not need to be encouraged to go on continuously rejoicing in the Lord?

The world reminds us that circumstances are not always conducive to rejoicing; but then the believer is "in Christ" and, therefore, our rejoicing is in Him. Had Paul merely said "rejoice," they might have tired hearing it.

A certain minister in my former home town in Pennsylvania was known to leave his sick and sorrowing parishioners with the parting words, "Keep your chin up!" Hearing this irksome, meaningless phrase in the hours of sorrow and suffering left the people with an empty void. The cleric was known in the community as "Mr. Chinnup."

Now Paul has something more than a phrase of false encouragement to offer the saints. He says: "Rejoice *in the Lord*." Circumstances may not at times be conducive to either peace or praise, yet the trusting saint can at all times rejoice in the Lord. The children of Israel were passing through much misery when Nehemiah reminded the remnant that "the joy of the Lord is your strength" (Neh. 8:10).

Are *you* in Christ? If you are, the apostle says to you, and to me: "Rejoice in the Lord alway: and again I say, Rejoice" (Phil. 4:4). Now remember, the simple formula for rejoicing always is "in the Lord." It is not in merely repeating the expression, but in realizing the experience. To those of us who are in Christ, Paul says, "Rejoice." Joy in the heart is the fruit of the Holy Spirit and is peculiar to those who are saved. It differs from the mirth and merriment of the world. This blessed fruit of the Holy Spirit's work in the heart is steadfast amidst poverty or plenty, sorrow or singing. Beloved, let us cultivate the joyful heart at all times.

B. *Resist the Enemy*

Secondly, "Beware." Paul is warning the saints to be on the alert.

There were three things for which they were to watch out. First, "Beware of dogs." The word "dog" is used often throughout the Scriptures, sometimes literally as in Luke 16:21, and at other times figuratively, as here. Several references illustrating its use figuratively will aid us in getting the apostle's thought.

Jesus said: "Give not that which is holy unto the dogs, neither cast ye your pearls before swine, lest they trample them under their feet, and turn again and rend you" (Matt. 7:6). Surely this does not mean that we should not give the gospel to the unsaved, as is sometimes interpreted. It seems that our Lord is using the word as does Isaiah, who said of the religious leaders of his day: "They are all ignorant, they are all dumb dogs, they cannot bark; sleeping, lying down, loving to slumber" (Isaiah 56:10). The use of the word by Isaiah, as in our Lord's passage, refers to mere religious professors who made professions because of gain to themselves. "They are greedy dogs which can never have enough, and they are shepherds that cannot understand: they all look to their own way, every one for his gain" (Isaiah 56:11). Jesus was saying that it is useless to discuss the things of the Spirit to professors who will not understand.

The Philippian believers were to watch out for any infiltration of legalism through Judaistic teachers who maintained the distinctive characteristics of the Jew's religion. The growth of Christianity gave rise to much concern among the Jewish leaders. In Paul's day there were Jews who were willing to go quite far in acknowledging Christ as a great prophet and teacher and accepting the high standard of Christian ethics, but they held fast to the one condition that the Law of Moses must not be violated. Actually those Jews were willing to assimilate Christianity with Judaism. But Paul would have nothing to do with reducing Christ to the level of Jewish prophets. No doubt the term "dog" in its earliest figurative use, was intended by the Jews to refer to the Gentile, but here the apostle uses it in a more general sense, applying it to Jews who professed to be Christians but who still considered it necessary to be bound by the Mosaic Law. In effect he is saying: "Watch out for the infiltration of mere professors."

In the Messianic psalm, depicting the sufferings of our Lord, we read: "For dogs have compassed Me: the assembly of the wicked have enclosed Me: they pierced My hands and My feet" (Psalm 22:16). It seems that here, as in Jeremiah 15:3, the word "dog" is used of those who would inflict cruelty. In Deuteronomy 23:18 the word is associated with that which is profane. In 2 Peter 2:22 the inspired writer, quoting from Proverbs 26:11, compares the dog with a foolish, sin-loving man (see also Revelation 22:15). Putting together these various usages, we may conclude that Paul is sounding a warning for the church at Philippi, and for all churches, to beware of any and all influences that might weaken the message of the gospel and turn away converts from the truth.

He continues, *"Beware of evil workers."* F. B. Meyer says that these are not the same as evildoers. A. R. Laurin says that there was no difference in character between "dogs" and "evil workers," the only difference being in method. The "dog" exemplifies devouring error with animal-like rapacity. The "evil worker" exemplifies deceitful tactics.

Meyer writes: "They are not set upon doing all the harm they can in the world, but are fanatical, unbalanced, and unable to distinguish between a part and the whole, magnifying some microscopical point in Christianity until it blinds the eye to the symmetry, proportion, and beauty of Heaven's glorious scheme. These people are the 'cranks' of our churches; they introduce fads and hobbies; they exaggerate the importance of trifles; they catch up every new theory and vagary, and follow it to the detriment of truth and love. It is impossible to exaggerate the harm that these people do."

The evil workers may hold to high standards of morality; nevertheless they are workers of iniquity. They are those of whom our Lord spoke when He said: "Beware of false prophets, which come to you in sheep's clothing, but inwardly they are ravening wolves" (Matt. 7:15). They may put their pious phrases in smooth language, but the Holy Spirit calls them "evil workers." It seems that Paul had in mind a particular people who would read this Epistle, and their activities were well known to those at Philippi. Any man who works against the gospel of grace is an evildoer.

A third warning concludes the precaution: "Beware of the concision." The word "concision" means "mutilation, cutting in pieces." It would seem that Paul is here using "concision" as a play on the word for "circumcision," for he follows it up by adding:

> For we are the circumcision, which worship God in the spirit, and rejoice in Christ Jesus, and have no confidence in the flesh.
>
> Phil. 3:3

The Judaizers could boast that they were circumcised according to God's covenant with Abraham, and even though they professed to believe in Christ, they insisted that all who confess Him must be circumcised according to the law. Is Paul ridiculing them by calling them the concision? At any rate, such circumcision is to the apostle nothing more than a mutilation of the flesh. They themselves profess to believe in Christ, but then they insist that circumcision of the flesh is essential to salvation. "And certain men which came down from Judea taught the brethren, and said, Except ye be circumcised after the manner of Moses, ye cannot be saved" (Acts. 15:1).

Paul calls such men mutilators, for their cimcumcision was worthless. Pagan worshipers mutilated their own bodies as did the prophets of Baal (1 Kings 18:28), and these Judaizers were guilty of the same when they added law to grace. True circumcision is a work of God in the heart (Rom. 2:25-29). Mere externalism is of no avail. Any ceremonial requirement for salvation is a defilement of the truth. Of all such externalities Paul warns to beware. Similarly, in our own day, we must beware of other forms of legalism, such as the demand for baptism, the Lord's Supper, fasting, the confessing of sins to men, as conditions of salvation.

Do we get the full impact of Paul's thrice-repeated warning? Do we feel its cumulative effects? As though he would build a great signboard to keep the believer on the highway of truth, he says: "Beware . . . beware . . . beware."

C. *Refrain from the Flesh*

Paul asserts the position he knows to be of God. Including the Philippian saints with himself, he says:

> For we are the circumcision, which worship God in the spirit, and rejoice in Christ Jesus, and have no confidence in the flesh.

> Phil. 3:3

The religion of the Judaizers was a religion of works, hence a religion of the flesh. The same must be said of all religions that add to, or subtract from, salvation by grace through faith in the Lord Jesus Christ. But there is a true circumcision that worships God in the spirit. Its only outward manifestations are the worship and work of a humble servant who rejoices in Christ Jesus. "In whom also ye are circumcised with the circumcision made without hands, in putting off the body of the sins of the flesh by the circumcision of Christ: Buried with Him in baptism, wherein also ye are risen with Him through the faith of the operation of God, who hath raised Him from the dead. And you, being dead in your sins and the uncircumcision of your flesh, hath He quickened together with Him, having forgiven you all trespasses" (Col. 2:11-13).

The act of circumcision was literally the cutting off of the flesh physically. The Judaizers had come to rest in this national and religious rite, having more confidence in it than in the finished work of Christ. Thus it became a corrupted ceremonialism. Paul explains that true circumcision is an inward work of the Holy Spirit. It is the setting aside of the self-life and placing one's self entirely in God's hands. Elsewhere Paul calls it co-crucifixion with Christ (Gal. 2:20; 6:14). There are three striking characteristics of the true circumcision:

First, "we worship God in the spirit." In contrast to the worship of the Old Dispensation, which was chiefly ritualistic in character, the true believer, having been born of the Spirit, from above, worships God inwardly. True worship is a matter of the spirit and not of the flesh. It does not take on certain outward forms nor prescribe to a specified ritual. Jesus said to the woman of Samaria: "God is a Spirit: and they that worship Him must worship Him in spirit and in truth" (John 4:24).

The body of the Christian becomes a temple in which God is worshiped in every thought and meditation and in the performing of every duty. So Paul writes: "I beseech you therefore, brethren, by the mercies of God, that ye present your bodies a living sacrifice, holy, acceptable unto God, which is your reasonable service" (Rom. 12:1).

Secondly, we who are of the true circumcision "rejoice [glory] in Christ Jesus." We ourselves have nothing to commend us for approval before God or man. We are saved by grace, disciplined by grace, and kept by grace. Left to ourselves we would fail utterly. When the twenty-four elders fell down before Christ's throne, they said:

"Thou art worthy, O Lord, to receive glory" (Rev. 4:11). Following this tribute the elders were joined by angels and living creatures numbering "ten thousand times ten thousand, and thousands of thousands; Saying with a loud voice, Worthy is the Lamb that was slain to receive power, and riches, and wisdom, and strength, and honour, and glory, and blessing" (Rev. 5:11-12). True Christians join Heaven's hosts in giving glory to Christ.

Finally, we "have no confidence in the flesh." The flesh is the old nature, the old self, and it can never be trusted. Paul testifies: "For I know that in me (that is, in my flesh,) dwelleth no good thing: for to will is present with me; but how to perform that which is good I find not" (Rom. 7:18).

The old nature in the believer is as corrupt and vile as the old nature in the worst sinner. The flesh never changes. Jesus said: "That which is born of the flesh is flesh" (John 3:6). God makes no attempt to improve it. The flesh is violently opposed to the Person and operations of the Spirit. "For the flesh lusteth against the Spirit, and the Spirit against the flesh: and these are contrary the one to the other: so that ye cannot do the things that ye would" (Gal. 5:17).

Beware, Christians, lest you become deceived by what appears to be a fair show of the flesh. None of us dare trust ourselves for one single moment. There is only one place for the old man, and that is on the cross. "And they that are Christ's have crucified the flesh with the affections and lusts" (Gal. 5:24).

XIII. PEDIGREE

Though I might also have confidence in the flesh. If any other man thinketh that he hath whereof he might trust in the flesh, I more:

Circumcised the eighth day, of the stock of Israel, of the tribe of Benjamin, an Hebrew of the Hebrews; as touching the law, a Pharisee;

Concerning zeal, persecuting the church; touching the righteousness which is in the law, blameless.

Philippians 3:4-6

In a clear and straightforward challenge to these Judaistic legalizers, Paul now sets forth a bit of his preconverted past, hoping to silence them somewhat. They had been insisting that in order to be saved, one must of necessity keep the Mosaic law in addition to his faith in Christ. He seeks to show them that if there is any acceptance with God from the standpoint of the Jews' religion, he himself would have surely obtained it. His argument is based upon his own pedigree as a Jew.

Though I might also have confidence in the flesh. If any other man thinketh that he hath whereof he might trust in the flesh, I more.

Phil. 3:4

The Judaizers trusted in the works of man for their salvation. That is, they had put their confidence in the flesh. Any such system of human effort is a natural system attempting to do something to satisfy the demands of God. It is at this point that Christianity differs from,

149

and stands uniquely above, all the religions of the world. Christianity is supernatural, purely a work of God, and thereby rules out of the picture entirely any taint of human merit and attainment, depending completely upon the merits of the only perfect sacrifice for sin, the Lord Jesus Christ. But for the sake of argument, or sound reasoning, Paul sets forth his pedigree to show that, if salvation could be had by human merit, he had more to boast in than they. And yet he gladly laid aside all of his attainments in order that he might receive salvation by grace through faith in Jesus Christ.

Paul mentions seven phases of his association with the Jews' religion. They may be likened to seven steps reaching to the heights of Judaism, and they make a striking contrast to the seven steps of Christ in His descent from the heights of Heaven to the humiliating depths of hell. Before we examine Paul's pedigree it will be good for us to keep before us his testimony in verse 7, "But what things were gain to me, those I counted loss for Christ." From those of us who have given up so little for Christ and His cause, a similar testimony would have little meaning. But in the case of Paul it stands out, to the mind of this writer, at least, as one of the most convincing testimonies ever to come from any Christian. As a Jew, Paul was justifiably proud of his past.

A. *Pride in Ritual*

"Circumcised the eighth day." Paul did not come into Judaism as a Gentile proselyte, nor was his circumcision administered later in life. It was according to the divine arrangement. God had said to Abraham: "This is My covenant, which ye shall keep, between Me and you and thy seed after thee; Every man child among you shall be circumcised. And ye shall circumcise the flesh of your foreskin; and it shall be a token of the covenant betwixt Me and you. And he that is eight days old shall be circumcised among you, every man child in your generation, he that is born in the house, or bought with money of any stranger, which is not of thy seed" (Gen. 17:10-12).

Every loyal Jew practiced the sacred rite of circumcision on the eighth day. Zacharias and Elisabeth brought John the Baptist to be circumcised the eighth day (Luke 1:59). Likewise Mary brought the infant Jesus for circumcision on the eighth day (Luke 2:21). This was according to the Mosaic law. "And the Lord spake unto Moses saying . . . in the eighth day the flesh of his foreskin shall be circumcised" (Lev. 12:1, 3).

Paul testifies that on the eighth day he received this initial rite. It was a rite of which every Jew could be proud, for it was to him a ceremonial cleansing as well as marking him an heir of the covenant. Ishmaelites were circumcised but not until they were thirteen years old. Paul never forgot that he was a Jew by birth, but now he testifies:

> But what things were gain to me, those I counted loss for Christ.
>
> Phil. 3:7

Many unsaved people today are leaning hard on the fact that they were sprinkled with water as an infant or confirmed by some denominational rite as a child, just as Saul of Tarsus leaned on his circumcision. While none of us dare set himself up as a judge, one wonders how many there will be in hell who are counting on some rite of their church to get them to Heaven. It is not until one becomes saved by grace through faith in Jesus Christ that he is willing to count such things loss.

B. *Pride in Relationship*

"Of the stock of Israel." Paul could trace his ancestry back to the patriarch Jacob. Israel was the real name for the nation, and to the sincere Jew it meant much. This relationship added dignity to his pedigree. He was no convert to Judaism, but a blood-born Jew of the original aristocracy. He was a descendant of the man to whom God said: "Thy name shall be called no more Jacob, but Israel: for as a prince hast thou power with God and with men, and hast prevailed" (Gen. 32:28).

It is not the blood of a man's ancestors that saves him and cleanses from sin, but the blood of Jesus Christ, God's Son. The Bible says: "But as many as received Him, to them gave He power to become the sons of God, even to them that believe on His name: Which were born, not of blood, nor of the will . . . of man, but of God" (John 1:12-13).

Many there have been since Paul's day who have thought to inherit eternal life because they were attached to a family name known to be Christian. It will be well for us all to know now that the grace of God does not flow through human veins. Paul was the possessor of a coveted relationship with Israel, but this too he was willing to let go for Christ.

C. *Pride in Respectability*

"Of the tribe of Benjamin." The tribe of Benjamin was known for its unwavering loyalty to the throne of

David when the ten tribes separated to divide the kingdom. This tribe was respected for its allegiance at a time when the majority were disloyal. The house of Judah was the divinely appointed kingly line (1 Kings 12:21; 2 Chron. 11:3), and in spite of the hardness of Rehoboam's heart, the tribe of Benjamin followed God's choice. After the nation was restored from the captivities, the tribe of Benjamin was held in high respect for its integrity and faithfulness.

Respectability is a noble trait in any family, but such an ancestral heritage will never put a sinner in good standing with God. You may have some right to be proud of such an inheritance, but keep such pride in its place. No family tradition or valor can change the sinful hearts of that family's descendants in the sight of God. It is true the holy city was within the borders of the tribe of Benjamin, but that could not make Paul a holy man before the Lord. To be a Benjamite was something in which the flesh might well be proud. And in this Saul of Tarsus did pride himself until he met Jesus Christ.

D. *Pride in Race*

"An Hebrew of the Hebrews." Paul traces his pedigree to the first Hebrew, Abraham himself. There was never a mingling with Gentile blood in his family. His mother and father were pure Jews. Though living at Tarsus and receiving his education there, he never departed from true Hebrew tradition. He was, as one writer says, "Hebraically Hebrew," not like the Hellenistic Jews who conformed to Greek language and customs. He was proud of his racial distinction.

But with all of his racial position and pride, Saul was a lost soul until he came face to face with Jesus Christ. Before his conversion he was much like many since his time who take great pride in being American, English, Russian, German, and so on, but who allow that pedigree to become a barrier between Christ and themselves. The gospel of Christ has a universal appeal and is designed by God to go into all the world to every creature. Let no man, regardless of his race, think that he does not need saving.

E. *Pride in Religion*

"As touching the law, a Pharisee." We dare not look upon the ancient Pharisee as he has come to be looked upon in our time. We think of a Pharisee as the personification of false pride, arrogance, and contempt, but actually the Pharisee of the oldest order in Israel stood for a morality of the highest and strictest kind. When others flagrantly violated the law, the Pharisees maintained careful obedience to it. They held the Word of God and the tradition of the elders in highest esteem. H. A. Ironside wrote: "Of the various Jewish sects existing in his day, the Pharisees were the most intensely orthodox."

Paul was as proud of his religious pedigree as he was proud of anything else. At least two times he bore witness to his being a Pharisee. As he stood bound before the council at Jerusalem, he said: "Men and brethren, I am a Pharisee, the son of a Pharisee" (Acts 23:6).

When on trial before Agrippa, he testified: "After the most straitest sect of our religion I lived a Pharisee" (Acts 26:5).

When our Lord stressed the need for practical righteousness He said: "For I say unto you, That except your righteousness shall exceed the righteousness of the scribes and Pharisees, ye shall in no case enter into the kingdom of heaven" (Matt. 5:20).

No one can lightly set aside religious convictions as those of the Pharisees, those orthodox defenders of the Mosaic law. But then one may be devoutly sincere in his religious convictions and at the same time be sincerely wrong. The world has in it many people who were proud of their religion until they received Jesus Christ. And then, like Paul, they saw the utter folly of holding to some tradition that was unable to save them from their sins. Now they testify with the apostle:

> But what things were gain to me, those I counted loss for Christ.
>
> Phil. 3:7

F. *Pride in Reputation*

"Concerning zeal, persecuting the church." Everybody who knew Saul of Tarsus knew how devoted he was to the Jews' religion and how intent he was in stopping the spread of Christianity. His movements were like a mighty hurricane. Luke describes him as "breathing out threatenings and slaughter against the disciples of the Lord" (Acts 9:1). So certain in his own mind was this zealot that he was right that he went about brutally stamping out the Christians in their own blood. We see him consenting to Stephen's death at the time of a great persecution against the Church (Acts 8:1). He had the reputation for being an honest and sincere protector of the Jewish religion. He was so completely overpowered by his zeal that he manifested a blind hatred against Christ and His Church.

Here was a man who worked hard at his religion. He felt it his religious duty to do so. He excelled in his reputation for practicing his religion. But with all of his zeal he was a lost sinner. "He measured his religious zeal by his hatred of Christians. We may do the same thing in a different way. Christians measuring their Christianity by their hatred of communism; fundamentalists measuring their fundamentalism by their hatred of modernists; Protestants measuring their Protestantism by their hatred of Romanists; and Romanists measuring their Romanism by their hatred of Protestants. It is a precarious reputation indeed which is measured by such standards." It is good to have a reputation if we are known for doing the right thing in the right way. But even a good reputation is a poor substitute for the salvation God offers in Jesus Christ. One glimpse of the Lord Jesus and Paul could say of his reputation:

> But what things were gain to me, those I counted loss for Christ.

> Phil. 3:7

G. *Pride in Righteousness*

"Touching the righteousness which is in the law, blameless." Here is a man who carried the righteousness of the law far enough so as to become blameless before men. It was not uncommon to find such men. We think of the young man who said to our Lord concerning the law, "Master, all these have I observed from my youth" (Mark 10:20).

Such claims set a man apart as being of great stature. Oh, he had sinned, but then he would bring the required

sacrifice in obedience to the ceremonial law and be pronounced clean. Paul was an unexcelled example of a
Jew who was ritually, respectably, racially, religiously,
reputably, and righteously correct in the eyes of all his
fellowmen.

But not until he was brought in contact with the glorified Christ did he learn the truth of the Old Testament
prophet that, "all our righteousnesses are as filthy rags"
(Isaiah 64:6). That day as he traveled the road to
Damascus he saw his pedigree as a filthy rag, a worthless
polluted garment. Until that crisis hour of his conversion
he had been going about to establish his own righteousness (Rom. 10:3), but Christ changed all of that. Later
Paul wrote: "For He [God] hath made Him [Jesus] to
be sin for us, who knew no sin; that we might be made
the righeousness of God in Him" (2 Cor. 5:21).

Now he no longer boasts in his pedigree but testifies:

But what things were gain to me, those I counted loss for
Christ.

Phil. 3:7

XIV. PERSPECTIVE

But what things were gain to me, those I counted loss for Christ.

Yea doubtless, and I count all things but loss for the excellency of the knowledge of Christ Jesus my Lord: for whom I have suffered the loss of all things, and do count them but dung, that I may win Christ,

And be found in Him, not having mine own righteousness, which is of the law, but that which is through the faith of Christ, the righteousness which is of God by faith:

Philippians 3:7-9

When a man's life undergoes an absolute spiritual transformation he has an altogether different perspective. His outlook is completely changed. From the hour of his regeneration he commences to re-evaluate life's values. It is quite probable that some things he formerly cherished as valuable will appear to be worthless, and in some instances harmful. It was just so with the Apostle Paul. Before his conversion he took great pride in the ritual of circumcision, his relationship to Israel, his respectability as a descendant of the tribe of Benjamin, his racial identification with the Hebrews, his religion as a Pharisee, his reputation as a zealot, and his righteousness as touching the law. But after he was born again through faith in Jesus Christ his whole outlook on life was changed. When his eyes met the gaze of God's Son, Paul turned his back on the balance sheet of former years. His testimony is most touching. It is a brand-new perspective.

A. *Past Decision*

But what things were gain to me, those I counted loss for
Christ.

Phil. 3:7

Reflecting upon the crisis hour in his experience when
he first met Jesus Christ, Paul recalls that initial decision.
He was the proud possessor of some choice assets, but as
he weighed these over against a life in Christ, he made a
definite surrender to the Son of God. He was willing to
forsake all to follow Christ. But before he could say "yes"
to the Lord Jesus, he had to be willing to lay aside those
things he held dear.

Moses, another mighty servant of God, and, like Paul,
a Jew, made a similar decision. "By faith Moses, when he
was come to years, refused to be called the son of
Pharaoh's daughter; Choosing rather to suffer affliction
with the people of God, than to enjoy the pleasures of
sin for a season" (Heb. 11:24-25).

No other pathway leads to a life of service for God.
We cannot cling to the old life and make the new life
count for Him. The "things" Paul surrendered were not
evil things. They were good in themselves but they were
not good enough to save him. A good thing can become a
bad thing if it keeps out the best thing. Even a man's
religion can damn his soul if he permits it to become a
substitute for Jesus Christ. Every man must make the
decision to surrender all, if need be, in order to be saved.
"Therefore if any man be in Christ, he is a new creature:
old things are passed away; behold, all things are become
new" (2 Cor. 5:17).

After serious contemplation Paul came to the settled conviction that Jesus Christ must have all. The apostle was not alone in this decision. Others before and since have experienced something of the same. Abraham was willing to sacrifice Isaac rather than disobey God. "By faith Abraham, when he was tried, offered up Isaac: and he that had received the promises offered up his only begotten son" (Heb. 11:17).

Mary gladly poured out her finest upon the Lord even though one accused her of waste (John 12: 3-6). Others said the same about Borden of Yale, Pilkington of Uganda, Studd of China, and many more choice servants of Christ who one day made that all-important decision to surrender all to Him. What is it that makes such absolute surrender possible? It is the correct answer to two questions: "Who art Thou, Lord?" and "What wilt Thou have me to do?" An experiential knowledge of Jesus Christ and His plan for my life should make me ready and willing to count all things loss, to cross everything off the books, and to begin life anew with Him. Many a child of God will testify that prior to his conversion he reckoned his worldly position and possessions to be an asset and Christ a loss, but now he reckons the righteousness of God in Christ his sole asset and all else, including his own life, a loss.

Every man is faced with just such a decision. We cannot hold on to our righteousness and our life and at the same time gain God's righteousness in Christ and His life. We simply cannot have both.

B. *Present Determination*

Yea doubtless, and I count all things but loss for the

excellency of the knowledge of Christ Jesus my Lord: for
whom I have suffered the loss of all things, and do count
them but dung, that I may win Christ.

Phil. 3:8

Paul's past decision, that initial act of surrender at the
commencement of his Christian experience, when he
counted loss "those things" that pertained to his racial
and religious background, was not all that he surrendered.
That was merely the beginning. With Paul it was a continuing attitude until he could say, "And now I count
all things loss." He testifies: "I *counted* those things loss
. . . I *count* all things loss." The two tenses of the verb,
past and present continuous, show that Paul persistently
pursued a life of sacrifice and surrender for his Lord.
When he wrote this Epistle, "all things" had been surrendered as worthless when compared with the all-surpass-
ing worth of his personal experience with Jesus Christ. He
completely revised his former standard of values. Weighing his losses and gains, he was more than pleased with
the results. To Paul, Christ makes all the difference in the
world. Surrender had cost him much but Christ brought
him gain.

The words "yea doubtless" might be translated "yes,
indeed," and they show the force and feeling of Paul's
convictions. He weighed carefully the possibility of holding on to those things and refusing Christ, but now that
he has appropriated Christ he is convinced that he is much
farther ahead. Yes, indeed, it will pay one well to forsake
all and follow Christ. James and John and Simon had a
prosperous fishing business going when they met Jesus,
but Luke says: "When they had brought their ships to
land, they forsook all, and followed Him" (Luke 5:11).

On one occasion they questioned whether they ought not to go back to the old way of life (John 21:3), but one day out of fellowship with Christ convinced them that He could bring them greater gain.

Ask the man who knows and he will tell you, "Yes, indeed, I am still reckoning all things to be of no value when compared with the excellency of the knowledge of Christ Jesus my Lord." The expression "the knowledge of Christ Jesus my Lord" refers to that knowledge Paul gained of Christ through personal communion with Him. Such knowledge is unexcelled. When a man really gets to know the Son of God, the glories of the old life have faded into oblivion. His gains in Christ overshadow any loss. After all, no man bemoans giving up something if he is certain to gain more. The bride on her wedding day counts all things but loss to gain her lover. The student counts all things but loss to gain the required knowledge for a successful career. It is a loss gladly suffered for the gain that is achieved.

Paul's experience in Christ was so blessedly real he was determined to pursue it to the end. His was a persistent determination. "I counted . . . I count . . . and do [continue to] count." The dividends accumulated from his new venture in Christ have come to him so regularly that he must press on. It is all so wonderful there can be no turning back. The farther on he went with his Lord, the less attraction the old life held for him. In fact, he used rather strong words when he says, "I count all things but dung." Turning with contempt upon those things he surrendered, he calls them "refuse," things to be cast to the swine. Would God we all had this spiritual sense of values! Some of us may think we know Christ but our false perspective of what is worthful shows up our ignorance. We may speak the language of one who knows the Lord intimately, but as long as we cling to the things of this world to the extent that they mar our vision of Him, we remain in ignorance and poverty.

C. *Personal Desire*

The life of a spiritual Christian is marked by progress. Having tasted something of the blessing in knowing Christ, his desire is to follow on for more of the same. Holy passions grip his soul so that there is before him that supreme desire to be more like his Lord. Paul held just such a desire. He writes:

> . . . that I may win Christ, And be found in Him, not having mine own righteousness, which is of the law, but that which is through the faith of Christ, the righteousness which is of God by faith.

Phil. 3:8-9

"That I may win Christ." The word "win" is the same Greek word translated "gain" in verse 7. He had renounced his gain to gain Christ. Having weighed the two, his desire now is always to have Christ for his gain. All other gains, social, financial, intellectual, political, are but small gains compared with the greatest gain. Having studied carefully that matter of profit and loss, the apostle desires nothing and no one other than Christ.

Paul's desire to gain Christ does not mean that he was not already saved, that he had not received Christ as his Saviour. Rather it is his desire to acquire and appropriate Christlikeness into his own life, such as Christ's self-sacrificing spirit, His humility, grace, forgiveness, and compassion. There are too many unyielded professing Christians whose so-called Christian experience stopped abruptly where it began, with a mere lip profession of Christ as Saviour. They show no desire to gain Christ. Is such a shallow profession truly Christian? I think not. Genuine Christianity goes far deeper than lip service. *"That I may . . . be found in Him."* Paul is not in doubt here as to whether or not he is really saved, nor is he doubtful or fearful about his future security. Actually Paul is drawing a contrast here between two righteousnesses, the Pharisaic righteousness of law observance, which characterized his former life, and the new experience of righteousness, which he received through faith in Christ. He calls them "mine own righteousness" and "the righteousness which is of God by faith." True righteousness has its origin with God. It cannot proceed out of the heart of man since the human heart is deceitful and incurably sick (Jer. 17:9). It is foolish to rely on a righteousness from man, since man can offer nothing acceptable to God. When the Holy Spirit shows a man his real self then he will say with the prophet of God: "But we are all as an unclean thing, and all our righteousnesses are as filthy rags; and we all do fade as a leaf; and our iniquities, like the wind, have taken us away" (Isaiah 64.6).

Paul is simply saying that he has no desire to return to his former religious views and practices. God's righteousness is better than his own; therefore, he would always be found in the God-created righteousness which saved him. The law-righteousness of the Pharisees is a self-righteousness which, while meeting certain social standards of men, can never reach God. Jesus said: "For I say unto you, That except your righteousness shall exceed the righteousness of the scribes and Pharisees, ye shall in no case enter into the kingdom of heaven" (Matt. 5:20).

The righteousness of the Pharisees was purely an external one wrought out by obedience to the law. The righteousness which will bring a man in right relation to God is both an imputed righteousness and an imparted one. God's righteousness is not merely a pronounced righteousness but an extremely practical one. God requires truth in the inward parts. The difference between God's view and man's view of righteousness can be summed up as follows: "For the Lord seeth not as man seeth; for man looketh on the outward appearance, but the Lord looketh on the heart" (1 Sam. 16:7).

The righteousness of man stands condemned because it cannot change his heart. Our Lord pronounces woe upon all self-righteousness. "Woe unto you, scribes and Pharisees, hypocrites! for ye are like unto whited sepulchres, which indeed appear beautiful outward, but are within full of dead men's bones, and of all uncleanness" (Matt. 23:27).

The apostle had learned that "the righteousness which is of God by faith" had changed him completely, inside and out, and that it opened the gateway to right living. Should he return to the old way of self-righteousness? Never! He describes his brethren after the flesh: "For they being ignorant of God's righteousness, and going about to establish their own righteousness, have not submitted themselves unto the righteousness of God" (Rom. 10:3).

God's righteousness requires no "going about" to establish one's self, but rather it is offered by His free unmerited grace. Paul abandoned his righteousness and gained God's righteousness in Christ, and now "in Him" he always would be found. His desire is to live that others might observe that he is in Christ. This was Paul's perspective.

XV. PURSUIT

That I may know Him, and the power of His resurrection, and the fellowship of His sufferings, being made conformable unto His death;

If by any means I might attain unto the resurrection of the dead.

Philippians 3:10-11

For some time now the pursuit of knowledge has been a major topic of conversation among top government officials and educators in our country. It all began when Russia was the first nation to launch a satellite into outer space. Our military and political experts became aware suddenly of the fact that the United States no longer held the leading position among the nations of the world in the pursuit of technical and scientific knowledge. Now the experts are going all-out in an endeavor to step up our educational program and to encourage our youth to pursue courses in science. I am not finding fault with this new interest in the pursuit for scientific knowledge. It seems to be a necessity when viewed from the standpoint of national security.

But when looked at in the light of eternal values it does seem a bit foolish to have to spend untold billions of dollars in an attempt to reach the moon first. When man arrives on the moon he will discover that he has but stepped from one tiny speck to another in God's vast incomprehensible universe, and that he is still lost in a howling wilderness. He will be no closer to God, and his knowledge will have gotten him nowhere. If our pursuit of scientific knowledge is necessary, our need to know God is infinitely greater.

I feel certain that the Apostle Paul was no ignoramus in his grasp of the arts and sciences in his day. Yet he held an aspiration that exceeded by far man's noble ambition to conquer outer space. However much Paul may have desired knowledge of the subjects pertaining to earth and its neighboring planets, his chief aim was to know the mighty Sovereign who created them all, including man. He expresses himself in these words: *"That I may know Him."* This is the transcendentalism of genuine Christianity. It is not a futile pursuit after the vague or the visionary, but it is the true teaching of the historic Christian position that man can attain knowledge which goes beyond or transcends pure reason.

The first step to a knowledge of God is a personal encounter with Jesus Christ. This must, of necessity, include the experiential knowledge of Christ as Saviour and Lord. Philip said to Jesus: "Lord, shew us the Father, and it sufficeth us." Jesus answered him, "He that hath seen Me hath seen the Father" (John 14:8, 9). Again He said: "He that seeth Me seeth Him that sent Me" (John 12:45). If a man would know God he must begin with Jesus Christ; he must know Jesus Christ. Paul expressed his aspiration by saying, "That I may know Him." Mark well the fact that he did not say, "That I may know *about* Him."

The average man of any intelligence and elevation of ideas about the teachings of Jesus will sympathize with you and possibly follow along in pursuit of knowledge about Him. But say to him that your aspiration is to know

Christ experientially in "the power of His resurrection, and the fellowship of His sufferings, being made conformable unto His death," and he will be bewildered at your babbling in an unknown tongue. Yet this was the high ambition of the great apostle who, in his day, could match wits with the philosophers of the schools of the Epicureans and Stoics (Acts 17:17-18). But had Paul been totally ignorant of philosophy and science, still with his knowledge of Christ he would have known more than they all who knew not Christ.

We cannot stress too emphatically that the word "know" means "to come to know by experience." Paul's aspiration is to come to know the Lord Jesus in that fullness of experimental and experiential knowledge by identifying himself with Christ and being like Him. Such learning is the highest kind of knowledge attainable, for experience is the best teacher after all. It is good to know about the Lord Jesus, but it is best to know Him by participation in a living experience. There is nothing shallow or superficial about the man who has set such knowledge as his goal in life. A knowledge about Christ received from reading a book or listening to a sermon could not satisfy the man in search of such a holy quest. Conformity to Christ is his goal and he refuses to stop short of it. It was this personal contact with life, and no mere intellectual knowledge, that our Lord had in mind when He prayed for His own: "And this is life eternal, that they might know Thee the only true God, and Jesus Christ, whom Thou has sent" (John 17:3).

How did Paul approach the realization of his aspiration? He sees the possibility of gaining a knowledge of Christ by a threefold experience.

A. *The Power of Christ's Resurrection*

Paul does not have in mind here the historical fact of Christ's Resurrection nor of his own resurrection after death. We must keep before us the fact that it is not a knowledge of history Paul is seeking but rather experience. At first it might appear that Paul is illogical in his reasoning. "That I may know Him, and the power of His resurrection, and the fellowship of His sufferings, being made conformable unto His death." "Resurrection . . . suffering . . . death!" Are these in their proper order? Should not the resurrection" appear last? If Paul is here speaking historically and chronologically then the arrangement is incorrect. But there is no mistake since the apostle is speaking experientially and psychologically. Christian experience commences with the believing sinner's tasting first of Christ's resurrection power in regeneration. Throughout the New Testament, conversion is described as a passing out of death into life. Jesus said: "Verily, verily, I say unto you, He that heareth My word, and believeth on Him that sent Me, hath everlasting life, and shall not come into condemnation; but is passed from death unto life. . . . Jesus said unto her, I am the resurrection and the life: he that believeth in Me, though he were dead, yet shall he live" (John 5:24; 11:25).

Writing to believers, Paul said: "And you hath He quickened [made alive], who were dead in trespasses and sins" (Eph. 2:1).

The first stage, then, in Christian experience is to receive new life, to be "born again" (John 3:3, 5). Saving faith begins with the Resurrection and produces spiritual life. "That if thou shalt confess with thy mouth the Lord Jesus, and shalt believe in thine heart that God hath raised Him from the dead, thou shalt be saved. For with the heart man believeth unto righteousness; and with the mouth confession is made unto salvation" (Rom. 10:9-10).

If all of the sinners who celebrated Easter day in the churches of their choice would have come to know the living Christ in salvation, I believe the world would have witnessed the greatest spiritual awakening in its history. We were born into this world spiritually dead, and nothing less that the lifegiving power of the living Christ can impart spiritual life. We can be saved only "if we believe on Him that raised up Jesus our Lord from the dead; Who was . . . raised again for our justification" (Rom. 4:24-25).

Since Paul was saved when he wrote this Epistle, surely he was not here expressing a desire to know Christ in His saving power. To what extent then did Paul desire to know Christ and the power of His Resurrection? The Christian life not only commences with the believing sinner's receiving the life of the risen Christ but it continues in exactly the same way. We are sustained by the same life that saves us. In his Ephesian letter Paul wrote: "That ye may know . . . what is the exceeding greatness of His power to usward who believe, according to the working of His mighty power, which He wrought in Christ, when He raised Him from the dead" (Eph. 1:18-20).

In ourselves we are too weak for the conflicts of life. If we are to conquer the daily habits of sin and live in holiness, we must draw from the power of Christ's risen life. We are now justified by His blood and reconciled to

God by the death of His Son; but then Paul adds: "We shall be saved by His life" (Rom. 5:9-10). To live in the power of Christ's Resurrection is to become more and more dead to the ways of the world and the lusts of the flesh, and to be more like Christ. "Likewise reckon ye also yourselves to be dead indeed unto sin, but alive unto God through Jesus Christ our Lord" (Rom 6:11).

The same power that raised up the Lord Jesus from the dead, works in the believer to provide victory in his daily life. It is God's unlimited power made available to us, if we want it. It was the experiential knowledge of that power, in its influence on his own inner life, that Paul pursued.

B. *The Participation in Christ's Sufferings*

Believers are united with Christ not only that they may share His life, but also that they may share His life and labor in behalf of others. We are called not only to enjoy His salvation but also to partake of His sufferings. Peter said: "Ye are partakers of Christ's sufferings" (1 Peter 4:13). There is no fellowship so precious as that which one has with a close and intimate friend in his sufferings. We share our joys with many, but our sorrows are shared with an intimate few. How many of us have come to know Christ in the sacred intimacy of His sufferings?

The "sufferings" of Christ mean not the physical pain and agony of the cross—in fact it is doubtful if Paul had in mind the actual sufferings of Christ's body at Calvary. The sufferings of the Cross, in which Christ bore the penalty for sins, He bore above. No other person could possibly share these with Him.

I believe the Scriptures hint as to what those sufferings may be to which Paul refers. When Paul was converted, our Lord said: "For I will shew him how great things he must suffer for My name's sake" (Acts 9:16).

The words "for My name's sake" may suggest a possible meaning of the "sufferings" Paul had in mind. Could it not be the suffering one must bear because of an all-out allegiance to Jesus Christ? There are sufferings in which we may have fellowship with our blessed Lord, such as being misunderstood, being the objects of the world's ridicule and persecution in our stand for Christ. Such suffering does not come to the Christian who has fellowship with the world. No believer who compromises his position in Christ can share in the fellowship of Christ's sufferings. Paul must have weighed fully the consequences of aspiring to such an experience. To know Christ in the fellowship of His sufferings meant to bear reproach for His Name's sake. Most of us would gladly enjoy the fellowship of Christ's blessings, but how many among us would just as gladly seek the fellowship of His sufferings? Have you ever prayed to God to ask Him that He would grant you the privilege of knowing Christ in the fellowship of His sufferings? Paul did!

Neither was the apostle thinking, in his request, of martyrdom for himself, but rather of that spiritual process that is carried on in the soul of a man who shares the Saviour's burden for a lost world. Our Lord suffered in His soul as He wept over Jerusalem. His heart was broken as He saw the multitudes as sheep having no Shepherd. Such anguish made up a substantial portion of His suffering. It was such suffering Paul longed to know in experience.

But no man is able to endure the fellowship of Christ's sufferings who does not know the power of Christ's Resurrection. All human effort fails before the sorrow and shame He bore. And yet it is possible for us to know just such a fellowship. More than this, it is only as we know something of the fellowship of our Lord's sufferings that we can be certain we know anything of the power of His Resurrection. Our belief in the literal Resurrection of Christ is not designed only to assure us a future resurrection. The power of Christ's Resurrection is vitally and essentially related to the Christian's experience in this life. It is that power in us now that enables us to know Him in the fellowship of His sufferings.

One who does not know Christ in the fellowship of His sufferings is not prepared to serve Him. He took upon Himself the form of a servant and was willing to be disowned by the world. He paid whatever price was necessary in order to be the Servant of all. Would you be one with Him in such an experience? Or are you satisfied to be one with the majority who mark out certain self-imposed boundaries whereby they serve as it suits their convenience? It can be doubted that the power of the resurrected Christ has worked a complete renewal in the heart of any man who has no desire whatever to fellowship in His sufferings.

C. *The Pursuit Ended*

Paul concludes his pursuit for knowledge with the expressed desire to be made "comformable unto *His death.*" "His death" was the goal of His incarnation. It marked the final stage of the purpose of His first Coming. Christ was born to die. He said: "The Son of man came not to be ministered unto, but to minister, and to give His life a ransom for many" (Matt. 20:28).

Now the apostle was not expressing a desire to die as Christ died, that is, on a cross, if need be. You will find Paul's meaning in such phrases as "crucified with Christ" (Gal. 2:20), "I die daily" (1 Cor. 15:31), and "always bearing about in the body the dying of the Lord Jesus" (2 Cor. 4:10). Being made conformable unto Christ's death is something we all shrink from. We do not surrender our lives easily; we die hard. We struggle frantically to keep the old man alive. But what does God's Word teach us? "Knowing this, that our old man is crucified with Him. . . . Likewise reckon ye also yourselves to be dead indeed unto sin, but alive unto God through Jesus Christ our Lord" (Rom. 6:6, 11). "For ye are dead, and your life is hid with Christ in God" (Col. 3:3).

This is the believer's true position in Christ and it was what Paul was striving for in daily practical experience. It was self-crucifixion that conditioned our Lord's entire earthly life and made it so fragrant and beautiful in the blessing of others. This is at once the deepest and the highest experience in life for Paul. It was not something Paul had to do, but something he wanted to do. It is not one of the divine imperatives; it is not one of the "musts." He said: "That I *may* know Christ." Obviously, spiritual attainment to the height that Paul aspired is a privilege and not one of the imperatives enjoined upon us. It is one of those things that await our decision. We may continue to live selfishly for this life only or we may renounce self and follow on to know the Lord.

But remember, our choice now will determine our

rewards in the next life. How apropos are our Lord's words as He concluded His discourse on the beatitudes! Hear Him: "Blessed are they which are persecuted for righteousness' sake: for their's is the kingdom of heaven. Blessed are ye, when men shall revile you, and persecute you, and shall say all manner of evil against you falsely, for My sake. Rejoice, and be exceeding glad: for great is your reward in heaven: for so persecuted they the prophets which were before you" (Matt. 5:10-12).

If we have a full account of Paul's life, then we have some idea of Paul's reward awaiting him at the Judgment Seat of Christ. And since each of us has a full account of his own life, we know what awaits us in that day. There is still time to pursue to know Christ and the power of His Resurrection and the fellowship of His sufferings, being made conformable unto His death.

And now let us conclude our present study with a brief examination of verse 11:

> If by any means I might attain unto the resurrection of the dead.
>
> Phil. 3:11

Clear your mind at once of any wrong ideas you may have as to Paul's being uncertain concerning the resurrection. There is no uncertainty here. Commenting on this verse, Ralph A. Herring writes: "Grammatically, the construction permits the idea of a difference in rank or order to which he aspires in the day of resurrection. It is not illogical that in a day of giving rewards some should take precedence over others, like honor students in commencement exercises." Obviously, there is something to which Paul wanted to "attain," but surely the resurrection itself is not attained by any works on our part. I am inclined to agree to the idea of attaining a reward rather than the actual resurrection itself.

A number of teachers have pointed out that this is the only place in the New Testament where this particular form of the Greek word for "resurrection" is used. Literally it means "the out-resurrection, the resurrection out from the dead ones." When the dead in Christ alone shall rise at His Coming in the air (1 Thess. 4:16), the giving of rewards will immediately follow. It was Paul's hope and desire that at the out-resurrection he might attain, that is, that he might receive, a reward for his pursuit of the knowledge of Jesus Christ. In order to receive that reward in the next life he would have to attain, or earn it, in this life. There are many dangers and many snares to prevent us from attaining. Beware!

The pursuit is ended. When a man dies to self and is made conformable to Christ's death, he has reached the apex of Christian experience.

XVI. PRIZE

Not as though I had already attained, either were already perfect: but I follow after, if that I may apprehend that for which also I am apprehended of Christ Jesus.

Brethren, I count not myself to have apprehended: but this one thing I do, forgetting those things which are behind, and reaching forth unto those things which are before.

I press toward the mark for the prize of the high calling of God in Christ Jesus.

Let us therefore, as many as be perfect, be thus minded: and if in any thing ye be otherwise minded, God shall reveal this unto you.

Nevertheless, whereto we have already attained, let us walk by the same rule, let us mind the same thing.

Philippians 3:12-16

Every sincere and honest Christian will admit two things. First, he will concede to past failure: that is, he has not realized the goal that God has set for His children. Secondly, he is not satisfied to remain in his present spiritual state. A sense of dissatisfaction is essential to development in one's spiritual life. When a Christian is satisfied that he has arrived, he ceases to grow. To admit that we have not attained lies at the root of our noblest attainments.

A. *An Honest Admission*

As Paul reviewed his past life and labors since becoming a Christian, the many converts he had influenced to Christ, the churches he had established, the large cities he reached with the gospel, surely he might have looked upon himself with a sense of satisfaction and a feeling of accomplishment. But honesty would forbid any boasting on his part. He would gladly admit that he had not attained to complete identification with Christ in the power of His Resurrection and the fellowship of His sufferings and conformability unto His death. He had made some progress but there was still much ground to be covered.

> Not as though I had already attained, either were already perfect. . . . Brethren, I count not myself to have apprehended.
>
> Phil. 3:12, 13

Here are the confessions of a truly great man. They express the realization that he had not reached the high-water mark of his calling. He was never fully satisfied with himself. Nor can any of us afford to be. Even if we have not sinned outwardly of late, we know the secret shortcomings of our hearts. We have not already attained nor can we count ourselves to have apprehended. It is said that Tennyson spent seventeen years writing "In Memoriam," that some parts he wrote as often as one hundred times, and then, when he released it to the publisher, he was dismayed by a feeling of dissatisfaction. Such a spirit is one of the secrets of true greatness.

The apostle would not have his readers draw a false conclusion that he felt he had reached the state of perfection. True, he had given up much for Christ's sake, but he had not yet arrived at the stage of perfect communion with Christ and perfect conformity with Christ's death. Nor will any believer ever attain unto it in this life. No matter how much we grow in knowledge and holiness, there will always be room for further development. At this point it will be good for us all to be reminded of a solemn warning: "Wherefore let him that thinketh he standeth take heed lest he fall" (1 Cor. 10:12).

A general truth to hold before us is the fact that every Christian is imperfect so long as he is on earth. Others may speak of us as examples of perfection, but you and I know ourselves to be very far from having reached perfection in our hearts. Others may have us marked as men of purity, patience, and practical godliness, yet we know our own hearts, that they are far from the standards that God has given to us. It is true that, amidst the glow and grandeur of first love, as young Christians we sometimes felt it impossible that we would ever sin against God. But we soon found out, as did Paul: "For I know that in me (that is, in my flesh,) dwelleth no good thing: for to will is present with me; but how to perform that which is good I find not. . . . I find then a law, that, when I would do good, evil is present with me" (Rom. 7:18, 21).

I believe that Paul, in the Philippian text, is admitting honestly that, in the measure of his true self-knowledge, he had not attained to perfection. But he is not satisfied to stand still.

B. *A Hearty Attempt*

But I follow after, if that I may apprehend that for which I also am apprehended of Christ Jesus.

Phil. 3:12

In closest connection with his realization of his own

imperfection, Paul is enthusiastic in his attempt to progress toward the goal. His is not the halfhearted effort of a dreamer. He is gravely serious and fervently earnest in his desire to "follow after." The words "follow after" come to us from a Greek word meaning "to pursue." It is a term that was used in connection with a sports event. Paul might have had in mind the image of a runner in competition. At the end of the course there is the goal, and with the end in view he presses down the track hoping to come in the winner. The judge sits at the goal ready to present the prize to the victor, and that is the prize Paul pursues. He does not bother looking to one side or the other in order that he might observe his competitors. The goal is his main objective.

One's duty to be diligent in the Christian life is set forth in many portions of the Word of God. By way of illustration the believer is said to be in a race. "Wherefore seeing we also are compassed about with so great a cloud of witnesses, let us lay aside every weight, and the sin which doth so easily beset us and let us run with patience the race that is set before us" (Heb. 12:1). "Know ye not that they which run in a race run all, but one receiveth the prize? So run, that ye may obtain. . . . I therefore so run, not as uncertainly; so fight I, not as one that beateth the air" (1 Cor. 9:24, 26).

The Christian life is compared with warfare. "Fight the good fight of faith" (1 Tim. 6:12). "I have fought a good fight" (2 Tim. 4:7). "For the weapons of our warfare are not carnal, but mighty through God to the pulling down of strong holds" (2 Cor. 10:4).

The Christian life is compared with a wrestling or boxing contest:

"We wrestle" (Eph. 6:12). "So fight I" (1 Cor. 9:26).

If we are true believers, the aim of spiritual progress will be a hearty attempt on our part to progress toward the goal. The finish line is marked "perfection," and though we may not arrive in this life, we dare not accept anything lower than this as our aim. Our being saved is merely the start of the contest. The late Guy H. King said: "This race is not just a sprint, not a quick, brisk burst of energy, and then done with. In that case, many more would have succeeded." It is a long-distance race, one that we must "run with patience" (Heb. 12:1). Too many of us have been like the Galatians of whom it was asked: "Ye did run well; who did hinder you?" (Gal. 5:7)

Why this continuous all-out effort?

If that I may apprehend that for which also I am apprehended of Christ Jesus.

The Lord laid hold of Paul for a definite purpose, so Paul would lay hold of that for which Christ laid hold of him. Now that God saved him, he cannot rest until he fully grasps the very purpose for which he was saved. He strives for a life that will leave no unfinished business when he is removed from this earthly scene. I do not believe there is anything that will compare with the realization that we have lived out the great purpose for which we were redeemed. On the other hand there is no tragedy so great as a Christian at the end of life's journey with the bitter knowledge that he failed to achieve that for which his Lord saved him. What shame there will be at the Judgment Seat of Christ for the Christian who missed the mark!

C. *A Holy Aspiration*

Brethren, I count not myself to have apprehended: but this one thing I do, forgetting those things which are behind, and reaching forth unto those things which are before,

I press toward the mark for the prize of the high calling of God in Christ Jesus.

Phil. 3:13-14

We come now to the secret of Paul's great success as a Christian. He was a specialist with singleness of purpose. One may not have surpassing ability or superior knowledge, but if he will concentrate there is no telling how far he can go. Paul had one burning passion; it was to achieve the goal as quickly as possible, and in order to accomplish this he would allow nothing to divert his attention from the "one thing."

You have observed that the words "this I do" are in italics, indicating that they are not in the original but were supplied by the translators. But are they needed? The literal rendering, "but one thing," seems to summarize the ideal as regards the purpose and pursuits of the Christian. Even in his prison cell the apostle's heart was fixed on one absorbing, overmastering devotion. He was concentrating on "one thing." Nothing is permitted to turn his heart from an all-out effort to know Christ and to make Him known. It was this "one thing" to which Mary was devoted when she sat at Jesus' feet to hear His word, and our Lord commended her by saying: "One thing is needful: and Mary hath chosen that good part, which shall not be taken away from her" (Luke 10:42).

Now the "one thing" is not the only thing a Christian will do, but rather it is the goal toward which everything he does will gravitate. Everything in life may help us to be more like the Lord Jesus. The routine work of every day, the periods for reading and study, the moments spent in rest and relaxation, the trials and suffering that may come to us, all must be used to achieve the goal of Christlikeness. When this "one thing" is always before us we will not respond unfavorably, no matter the nature of the circumstance that comes to us. All must contribute to conform us unto the image of Him whose we are and whom we serve. To this we are divinely chosen by God. "For whom He did foreknow, He also did predestinate to be conformed to the image of His Son" (Rom. 8:29).

To achieve the goal there are some things we must forget—*"forgetting those things which are behind."* It is possible that the memory of the past, in some things, might contribute toward our coming nearer the goal. Robert Johnstone has said that "the remembrance of sin is fitted to humble, of mistakes to suggest wiser courses, of mercies to encourage." But if we return to the illustration of the contestant in a race, the runner's progress would be hindered were he to take his mind off the goal to concentrate on his opponent. Even so, the Christian may not concentrate on the shattered hopes and deferred plans of the past, nor should he be slowed down in his progress by reflecting on past sins, so long as things have been made right with God and man. In Philippians 1:3 the apostle said: "I thank my God upon every remembrance of you." It takes a spiritually sound mind to remember that which edifies and to forget that which hinders.

Quoting Sir William Osler, R. A. Herring says, "The load of tomorrow added to that of yesterday, and carried today, makes the strongest falter." With many of us that tendency to live in the past prevails. We either rest on some accomplishment as though we have arrived, or else we live in the sagging spirit of regret over past failures. Forget the past and press on with the determination that each new day will find you more like Christ. Never look back on your past in such a way that it impedes further progress. Retrospection can be very depressing. Jesus said: "Remember Lot's wife" (Luke 17:32), of whom Moses wrote: "But his wife looked back . . . and she became a pillar of salt" (Gen. 19:26). There is no bright future for the Christian who wastes time dwelling on the past.

On the contrary, the apostle stretches forward to what lies ahead. This is the meaning of the words "reaching forth." Once in the race the runner must stretch every muscle and nerve as he pushes forward toward the goal. Are we straining ourselves to be like Christ? Beloved, it is given to each of us to fix the eyes steadfastly upon our blessed Lord, "looking unto Jesus" with all the devotion and dedication of the soul. It is better on ahead, for there are "those things which are before": namely, Paul's expressed ideal of attaining to the knowledge of Christ as set forth in verse 10.

The race of life makes big demands upon us. No flabby, ill-conditioned athlete ever won a race. Nor can the Christian expect to attain if he does not condition himself. "Wherefore seeing we also are compassed about with so great a cloud of witnesses, let us lay aside every weight, and the sin which doth so easily beset us, and let us run with patience the race that is set before us, looking unto Jesus" (Heb. 12:1-2).

The "race" is the life of faith and obedience, that pursuit of personal holiness that ever looks to the Saviour. The prime requisite for running well is not that of speed, but of rigorous self-discipline and vigorous endeavor, that we might reach the goal of victory over the power of indwelling sin, and perfect conformity to the lovely likeness of Jesus Christ. So that we may achieve the goal we are exhorted to "lay aside every weight," that is, we must get rid of every ounce of surplus flesh, train down to the least minimum. Some Christians choose to retain a superfluity of weights and cling to some besetting sin, and then they have the audacity to complain about how hard it is to get along as a Christian. The race of life is a lengthy one, extending throughout the whole of our earthly experience, and it calls forth everything that is within us.

D. *An Honor Achieved*

I press toward the mark for the prize of the high calling of God in Christ Jesus.

Phil. 3:14

Christlikeness is the ultimate in our redemption. At His appearing the goal will have been reached for every Christian (1 John 3:2), but the garland or crown for which we run will not be won by all. Only those who have pressed on toward the goal of perfection will be awarded the prize. Paul was paying a price for his faith in Christ as he penned this Epistle, but with persistency of purpose he keeps pressing toward the mark that he might win. The prize is before him. There is no higher honor than to achieve it since there is no higher calling than "the high calling of God in Christ Jesus."

Are we looking toward the finish of the contest? Do we realize that we must all stand before the Judgment Seat of Christ to be judged for these lives of ours since we were saved? I fear that some of God's dear children have strayed off the course and are not running on the divinely marked-out track. If we are to achieve an honor we must follow the rules, for "if a man also strive for masteries, yet is he not crowned, except he strive lawfully" (2 Tim. 2:5). And so Paul lived with the end in view, and when the hour of death confronted him, he could say: "For I am now ready to be offered, and the time of my departure is at hand. I have fought a good fight, I have finished my course, I have kept the faith" (2 Tim. 4:6-8).

Christian, be a specialist. Seek to know Christ as the "one thing" for which you live; if you do, life will hold less grief and disappointment for you.

Some years ago I heard Dr. Samuel M. Zwemer say that "the smaller the circumference of my thinking, the shorter the diameter of my mistakes." Now here is a bit of sound scriptural philosophy. Narrow down your thinking so as to concentrate more on Christ and less upon the things of this world, and you cannot lose. No higher honor can be achieved by any man than the distinction of hearing the Lord say: "Well done!"

And now in conclusion Paul appeals to the brethren to be "thus minded."

Let us therefore, as many as be perfect, be thus minded: and if in anything ye be otherwise minded, God shall reveal even this unto you.

Nevertheless, whereto we have already attained, let us walk by the same rule, let us mind the same thing.

Phil. 3:15, 16

There were those who shared with Paul those things he had discussed in the Epistle. He refers to them, and to himself, as being "perfect." In verse 12 he writes: "Not as though I . . . were already perfect." There is no contradiction here. But how are we to understand this seeming inconsistency? Kenneth Wuest says: "The answer is found in the fact that in verse 12 Paul is speaking of a finished process and absolute spiritual maturity beyond which there is no room for improvement, whereas in verse fifteen he is speaking of relative spiritual maturity where there is room for development and growth. This is clear from the fact that in the former verse he uses a verb in the perfect tense, whereas in the latter, he used a noun. Paul therefore exhorts the Philippian saints who are spiritually mature to consider themselves so only in a relative sense, and to remember that there is much room for growth in their lives." Herewith he calls upon the saints, those who are perfect in Christ in principle and position, to strain forward by purposeful practical maturity.

And if there be those who are "otherwise minded," that is, those who are not all-out Christians, God Himself will show you how foolish they are and how profitable it is for you to continue in the race. Regardless of the mediocrity of some, let us continue to move forward by the same rule, the divine measure by which we determine what is right. This rule is the Word of God and it alone must be our guide. So let us keep on stepping where the light of divine truth is shed upon our pathway. Never retreat; never turn back no matter how many there be that do so.

In closing permit me to pass on a word just received from my friend Dr. E. Schuyler English. He was traveling around the world and sent home the following:

> "Looking through the porthole of our cabin early in the morning, as the 'Kungsholm' approached Padang Bay, Bali, we were able to see majestic Genung Agung, one of the highest mountains in Indonesia, its peak rising 10,000 feet into the blue, cloudless sky. We wondered how many times its summit had been reached and whether anyone had lost his life in the attempt. This brought to mind something a friend in England told us several years ago.
>
> In a small churchyard at the foot of one of the great mountains of Switzerland, the body of a young Englishman, who was killed while making an ascent, is buried. On the tombstone, under his name and the dates of his birth and death, the following inscription is carved: 'HE DIED CLIMBING.' "

May that be true of each of us when the Lord comes for us or calls us. With the Apostle Paul we should long to be found "reaching forth unto those things which are before, [pressing] toward the mark for the prize of the high calling of God in Christ" (Phil. 3:13-14).

XVII. PERFECTION

Let us therefore, as many as be perfect, be thus minded:
and if in anything yet be otherwise minded, God shall reveal
even this unto you.

Nevertheless, whereto we have already attained, let us
walk by the same rule, let us mind the same thing.

Brethren, be followers together of me, and mark them
which walk so as ye have us for an ensample.

(For many walk, of whom I have told you often, and now
tell you even weeping, that they are the enemies of the cross
of Christ:

Whose end is destruction, whose God is their belly, and
whose glory is in their shame, who mind earthly things.)

For our conversation is in heaven; from whence also we
look for the Saviour, the Lord Jesus Christ:

Who shall change our vile body, that it may be fashioned
like unto His glorious body, according to the working
whereby He is able even to subdue all things unto Himself.

Philippians 3:15-21

Nothing hinders the testimony of Jesus Christ more
than disharmony among Christians. Paul was acquainted
with this problem in the churches, hence his frequent
appeals for unity of spirit. It seems that we are never
free from those divisive tendencies that creep in among
us. A part of the second chapter is directed against such
tendencies. "Be likeminded, having the same love, being
of one accord, of one mind. Let nothing be done through
strife or vainglory. . . . Do all things without murmurings
and disputings" (2:2-3, 14). Here in the section before
us the apostle deals once again with the problem.

A. *Exhortation*

Let us therefore, as many as be perfect, be thus minded: and if in any thing ye be otherwise minded, God shall reveal even this unto you.

Phil. 3:15

There is seeming difficulty surrounding the use of this word "perfect." In verse 12, Paul says: "Not as though I had already attained, either were already perfect. . . ." Here he speaks of the final perfection which is the goal of our redemption at the appearing of our Lord Jesus Christ when "we shall be like Him" (1 John 3:2). This is the believer's expectation, as we shall see when we come to verse 21 in our present chapter. Paul had little patience with the false teaching of sinless perfection in this life. At no time does he infer that he had already "arrived." But if he denies perfection in verse 12, how then does he number himself among the perfect in verse 15?

Here we have the grand paradox of perfection and imperfection, maturity and immaturity. It is a work of the mature mind that recognizes its immaturity. Only the fool will boast that he knows all, and nowhere does he reveal his folly more than in such a boast. We are moving toward perfection as we recognize our imperfections and seek to get rid of them.

But what does Paul mean when he says, "Let us therefore, as many as be perfect, be thus minded"? The word "perfect" (*teleios*) signifies having reached its end. It is a relative term used of physical development, wanting nothing.

"Of a little baby you exclaim, 'Isn't he perfect?' Yes, for his age and stage. You meet a fine, clean, healthy, upstanding fellow, and you remark, 'Isn't he a perfect specimen of young manhood?' Yes, for his age and stage: but he has a long way to go yet, for unless he grows, he will not be counted perfect of adult middle-age. You come across an old gentleman, kindly, unselfish, helpful, wise, sunny, and someone says, 'What a perfect old dear!' Yes, for his age and stage. Down on the running track, final perfection of the sprint is one hundred yards in ten seconds. You stand with stop watch in hand, and you gauge him at ten yards in one second —perfect: not final, but stage-perfect. So he goes on perfect at each ten yards' stage, until at the end of the hundred yards, he has reached final perfection at ten seconds. So is it with the New Testament—it is relative. When our Lord says, 'Be ye therefore perfect, even as your Father which is in heaven is perfect' (Matt. 5:48), He does not mean that we are expected to attain divine perfection; but that we are to be perfect in our sphere, and stage, as God is in His." (Guy H. King).

Looking further at our Lord's words in Matthew 5:48, He commands His followers to be perfect in a relative sense. He is teaching them how to behave toward their enemies. He said: "Love your enemies, bless them that curse you, do good to them that hate you, and pray for them which despitefully use you, and persecute you" (Matt. 5:44). And then he adds: "Be ye therefore perfect, even as your Father which is in heaven is perfect."

In their attitude toward their enemies they were to duplicate that of the Father. In this they were to be perfect; they were to be mature. There are, then, some things in which the believer can be perfect, not finally perfect in all stages, but perfect in certain phases and stages of Christian experience. Paul and his brethren at Philippi were not yet perfect in all stages, but they were spiritually mature in a relative sense, with much room for spiritual growth in some areas in their lives.

"Let us therefore, as many as be perfect, be thus minded." Here he speaks directly to the *"thus minded,"* the spiritually mature ones who share Paul's mind on those matters he has been discussing: namely, that he did not believe in sinless perfection and that he had not already attained to it. Paul regarded himself spiritually as an adult (1 Cor. 13:11), and in this he associated others with him, but he recognized that both he and they had much to learn. Those who have reached a stage of perfectness, or maturity in Christian experience, are to continue on in obedience as they have done in the past, using the same means of growth. An apple may have matured in size by July, but it does not reach the final stage of perfection in ripeness until the season runs its course, possibly in late August or September. Thus it must remain in closest contact with its source of life, the tree, until the end of its season. There is a maturity that marks the full-grown man in Christ in contrast with the babe in Christ, but even the mature Christian must keep in close touch with the source of spiritual life until the end of his season when he has run his course.

No doubt the apostle, in referring to the "thus minded," has in mind those "that are of full age" in contrast to that one who is a "babe" (Heb. 5:11-14), the "men" in contrast to the "children" (1 Cor. 14:20), the babes who are "yet carnal" in contrast to the "men" who are "spiritual" (1 Cor. 3:1-3). There are different stages of development in Christian growth, designated by the Apostle John in the following terms: "little children," "young men," and "fathers" (1 John 2:13, 14). Some Christians have grown in spiritual stature to be as "fathers"; others have a certain spiritual vitality to be as "young men"; while still others, for all their many years as Christians, are yet "little children."

A little boy was put snugly to bed by his mother. A few moments after he went to sleep he fell from his bed to the floor. Hearing the sound, mother came running to the child's room and asked him how he came to fall out of his bed. The lad replied: "I don't know, mummie, unless it was I went to sleep too near where I got in." The spiritually immature have gone to sleep too near where they got in. Watch out! You are in for a fall. We must press on. Paul is addressing himself to the fathers in the faith, rich in faith and ripe in grace, but still pressing on.

These two usages of the word "perfect," as set forth in our Philippian passage, are used similarly by Paul in Ephesians. "And he gave some [to be], apostles; and some, prophets; and some evangelists; and some, pastors and teachers; For the perfecting of the saints, for [unto] the work of the ministry [of ministering], for [unto] the edifying [building up] of the body of Christ: Till we all come in the unity of the faith, and of the knowledge of the Son of God, unto a perfect [fullgrown] man, unto the measure of the stature of the fulness of Christ" (Eph. 4:11-13).

There is that "perfecting of the saints for the work of the ministry"—a continuous process which is going on in our hearts at all times. Then there is the final perfection toward which the former is working, seen in the "perfect man" who arrives at the stature of the fulness of Christ, perfect as only He is perfect. The final perfection will be realized at His Coming when we shall be like Him (1 John 3:2).

"And if in any thing ye be otherwise minded, God shall reveal even this unto you." Having spoken first to the thus minded," the apostle now addresses himself to any who may be "otherwise minded." Some obviously had disagreed with Paul, and although sincere, they could not see the necessity of an all-out sacrifice as Paul saw it (verses 13-14). He has no desire to argue about it. If others felt they had arrived and were already perfect, the apostle merely says that God shall make known to them all such matters. He will trust the Lord to clear up the differences between them. Sound reasoning and patience on the subject of Christian perfection is needed because of the two extremes of antinomian license and professed perfectionism, because of the differences of temperament, heredity, environment, education, and circumstances of varied kinds. But to all who are striving honestly to know the mind of God, Paul reminds them that God shall reveal it to them. Jesus said: "If any man will do His will, he shall know of the doctrine, whether it be of God, or whether I speak of Myself" (John 7:17).

How patient we need to be with one another on matters about which no man can be dogmatic! Where there is a willingness to be taught of God, we can depend upon the Holy Spirit to guide the believer into all truth. It is unfortunate that we should have in our local assembly both the "thus minded" and the "otherwise minded." I trust that among us there will not be the "otherwise minded" who think they have reached the place beyond which there is no room for spiritual development and progress in Christian experience. However, I am convinced in my own heart that we all should feel the need and the urge to progress in holiness as strongly as did Paul.

> Nevertheless, whereto we have already attained, let us walk by the same rule, let us mind the same thing.
>
> Phil. 3:16

The knowledge Paul had and the progress he had made were the result of walking the royal road of divinely-revealed truth. Now he calls upon his own soul and exhorts the brethren to "walk by the same rule." In other words, the present duty of every believer is to obey the light God has given him. As Christians we must be of one mind in being true to the light we have already attained. Paul exhorts all those who, along with himself, would pursue the course of pressing toward the mark for the prize of the high calling of God in Christ Jesus to continue on in the race, to live unitedly the great truths that had been learned. When two or more persons walk by the same measuring rod they are in step with each other.

My own heart is exercised over you to whom God has called me to minister. Beloved, we have not arrived as yet. There is progress to be made. As far as we have come by God's leading, let us keep ourselves in the same path. Anything that would interfere with our running the race well we must let go. If on these things we can agree, the Word of God will both draw and keep us together. But remember, we must have the same prize in view as our goal.

H. E. Anderson tells how he came across an acquaintance he had not seen for many years. They talked together of the past, but Mr. Anderson was interested also in hearing of his friend's present work, for in the conversation the man had mentioned that he was engaged in some important literary translating. It seems that he possessed some land in a certain English country, but others were laying claims to it. He was fighting the claim, as the land had been discovered to be particularly rich in minerals. He said, "If I can only establish my claim it may mean sixty or seventy thousand pounds to me." He then told Brother Anderson that for months he had been reading the ancient deeds which went back hundreds of years. They were written in crabbed Latin and were most difficult to decipher. Day after day, night after night, he had been at work. No sacrifice, no strain was too great, for a valuable prize was in view.

Beloved, we too have a prize in view, perfection in our Lord Jesus Christ. Ours must be a life of progress in holiness, and the reward is on ahead. We dare not think for one moment that we have realized in this life all there is for us, and like the Laodiceans boast that we "have need of nothing" (Rev. 3:17). Let us hold to the simplicity of the passage before us, walking by the same rule and minding the same things, and it will pay rich dividends when we meet our Lord face to face.

> "It is the old story of diverted desires as narrated in the tale of the golden apples. Atalanta was a maiden of passing beauty and exceeding swift of foot. Her hand in marriage was offered to the Greek who would beat her on the course. Many tried and failed, and, as a consequence, forfeited their lives. At last Hippomenes ventured his fate, and set off from the mark with the maiden close on his heels. As she was about to pass him he threw out on the course a glittering golden ball. Atalanta pounced after the toy while the youth shot

ahead. Again she overtook him, and again he enticed her from the course. A third time he played his trick on her, and as she bounded after the bauble he passed the judge's seat, won the race, escaped death, and claimed his bride. Not by the superior speed of her opponent was Atalanta overcome but by her own folly in leaving the course for a mere toy. And has it not often been the undoing of a saint in the more glorious race that, for the trifling prizes of the world's offering, he has turned aside, become absorbed in the secondary, because of mundane affairs, and so has had his speed impeded, if not altogether stopped?"

No doubt there have been many Christians who have been lured off the main course of life by some attraction of this world only to find themselves in a struggle of rivalry and competition for worldly gain, with no other end in view but wealth or fame. How foolish to allow one's self to become sidetracked! In conclusion, I must stress the apostle's exhortation by saying that however far we have come by the Word of God, let us pursue the same path.

B. *Example*

Brethren, be followers together of me, and mark them which walk so as ye have us for an ensample.

Phil. 3:17

John Newton is reported to have said: "I have ever to confess, with sorrow, that I am far from being what I ought to be, and far from what I wish to be, but also— blessed be God's name!—to testify that I am far, very far, from what I once was." This testimony is not that of a braggart nor is it inconsistent with genuine Christian humility. Here is but an observation, upon self-examination, of both human weakness and, at the same time, the matchless grace of God. Certainly it is not wrong for a child of God to keep a check on himself as to his progress in Christian experience. Every man, without thought or intention or consciousness of it, is ever an example that someone else will follow. As Christians we need to know exactly what kind of example we are setting for others. And remember, we are setting a pattern for others, and others are following us even though they are not conscious of any influence exerted nor we of any followed.

Paul was aware of the fact that he was an influence upon the lives of others, so much so that he solicited careful observation from Christians young in the faith. To the Corinthians he said: "Wherefore I beseech you, be ye followers of me" (1 Cor. 4:16).

You can see at once the close connection between verses 15 and 16. Through the gospel that Paul preached to them, a spiritual relationship had been established between him and them. Knowing that they would be influenced by someone, either the would-be teacher at Corinth or else by others, he urges them to imitate him. A child may have many teachers or tutors, but they will not have the position that the child's father holds. Paul expects the young Christians at Corinth to follow his example even as a father might expect his own son to do. But lest they mistake his concern for them to be pride in his own heart, he adds: "Be ye followers of me, even as I also am of Christ" (1 Cor. 11:1).

Actually Paul is not pointing to his own example as such, but he asks the Corinthians to be his imitators only insofar as he imitates Jesus Christ. This verse obviously is a part of the end of chapter 10. Paul is not advertising himself, nor is he setting up himself as an example, but he is lifting up Christ. Christ is the ultimate standard, and they are to follow the Lord. A Christian must be living mighty close to his Lord to speak as the apostle did. It is as though he were saying. "Now I want your life to be a good testimony for your Lord." And then they replied, "But we do not know what to do in order to accomplish this." At this point he besought them to follow him in his life and teachings as he followed Christ.

What a challenge we have here to parents, pastors, Sunday school teachers, youth counselors, and others. The children and young people in our homes and assemblies are consciously or unconsciously following the examples we set. We set the pace and shape the pattern by our lives. We form the mold and fashion the model for others, thus they will become imitators of us as did the Thessalonians of Paul (1 Thess. 1:6). How important then that we be able to testfy: "Ye are witnesses, and God also, how holily and justly and unblameably we behaved ourselves among you that believe" (1 Thess. 2:10).

Recently my wife was asked to speak to a women's missionary union in the city of Detroit. She was assigned a subject that dealt with the problem of why so few of our Christian young people are offering themselves to Jesus Christ for Christian service. Only one week before the invitation came to her, our older son had graduated from Dallas Theological Seminary and had been called to the pastorate of the Fort Worth Bible Church, in Fort Worth, Texas. Mrs. Strauss wrote at once to our son asking him what it was that influenced him most in making his decision to devote his life to Christian service. It was both informative and interesting to read his reply. From early childhood he had followed a pattern that was set by the behavior of others.

The word that Paul uses for "ensample" in Philippians 3:17 is *tapor*, and its primary usage had reference to an impression, or mark, made by a blow. It was the impress or figure made by a seal or die. It was the word Thomas used of our Lord when he said: "Except I shall see in his hands the print [the impression] of the nails, and put my finger into the print of the nails. . . . I will not believe" (John 20:25). To Thomas the marks of crucifixion were all he had to go by, and all other impressions were to him false. Unless we are imitators of Christ, we leave false impressions with others as to what Christianity really is. The impressions we make are the results of a die already cast. Elsewhere Paul wrote: "From henceforth let no man trouble me: for I bear in my body the marks of the Lord Jesus" (Gal. 6:17).

The word "marks" is translated in the Revised Version as "brands." Some brand marks, or impressions, had already been made upon Paul, and those impressions were what others were seeing when they looked at him. Since they were "the marks of the Lord Jesus," the apostle could say, "Brethren, be followers together of me." Paul carried enough scars on his body to place his loyalty to Christ beyond question. Any Christian who is ashamed to bear suffering or reproach for our Lord's sake is a poor example and one not to be followed.

The apostle did not stand alone as an excellent example to be followed, for he adds: "and mark them which walk so as ye have *us* for an ensample."

Seemingly he included Timothy, Epaphroditus, Silas, and others known in the church at Philippi. There were those who should be marked or observed so as to be avoided, but then there were others, like himself, who shared Christ's likeness and whose Christian conduct was commendable. This was the pattern to be followed. Paul's own example, which he suggested they imitate, is recorded in verses 7-14. Such a life can call forth imitation by others.

In closing this portion of our study which deals with Paul the example, another passage comes to mind which is worthy of consideration at this point. "This is a faithful saying, and worthy of all acceptation, that Christ Jesus came into the world to save sinners: of whom I am chief. Howbeit for this cause I obtained mercy, that in me first Jesus Christ might shew forth all longsuffering, for a pattern to them which should hereafter believe on Him to life everlasting" (1 Tim. 1:15-16).

Paul considered himself the recipient of God's mercy that he might be a "pattern"; thus his whole life, subsequent to his conversion, was dedicated to presenting to others an outline sketch of what a Christian should be. God saved Paul in order that he might show by the example of his conversion that what Jesus Christ did for him He can and will do for others. Was not this the special object our Lord had in view in extending His mercy to you and me? I believe He has saved us to be a pattern to all future believers. Are we serving as examples of those who have been saved by His grace? May it be so!

C. *Enemies*

For many walk, of whom I have told you often, and now
tell you even weeping, that they are the enemies of the
cross of Christ:

Whose end is destruction, whose God is their belly, and
whose glory is in their shame, who mind earthly things.

Phil. 3:18-19

Not all are examples of what a true Christian ought
to be. It is a sad state of affairs that there are many who
are "the enemies of the cross of Christ." I say it is a sad
state of affairs when men oppose all for which the Cross
of Christ stands, for it caused the great apostle deep
emotion and tears. This is not Paul's first warning in this
Epistle against such, for he spoke of these enemies as
"dogs" and "evil workers" (3:2). They may have professed that they were Christians. However, they were of
the opposition in disguise, wolves in sheep's clothing
(Matt. 7:15), dogs and sows pretending to be chiefs (2
Peter 2:22). Professing Christians who use Christianity
as an excuse for lawlessness are a threat to the testimony
of the Church. To have to write so severely of professed
followers of Christ brought tears to Paul's eyes. These
were not drunkards and harlots that caused him to weep,
but men who said they were Christians.

In contrast to men like Paul and his godly companions,
the Church must contend with this peril which is one of
the greatest hindrances to the progress of Christianity.
When a man speaks the language of the Church and pro-
fesses to be a part of her life and labors and at the same
time is an enemy of her very foundation, he inflicts
greater havoc than does a Bertrand Russell (and his

kind) who wrote his book, *Why I Am Not a Christian.*
These internal enemies "would pervert the gospel of
Christ" (Gal. 1:7), and in so doing will "trouble you."
The apostle will now expose them in four severe and
denunciatory statements. And lest you feel he is lacking
in grace and tenderness, remember he weeps as he writes.

"Whose end is destruction." The word for "destruction"
in the Revised Version is "perdition," indicating a loss
of well-being, not of being. Judas was called by our Lord
"the son of perdition" (John 17:12) because he was a
child of Satan and would therefore suffer the utter loss
of blessedness in the future state while suffering eternal
misery. Perdition is the direct antithesis of salvation. It
awaits all unbelievers and, as indicated in our passage,
especially those who make a profession of Christianity
but who have not been born again. In this instance the
judgment fits the offense. In contrast to the true children
of God who glory in the Cross (Gal. 6:14), these are
Christ's enemies to whom the preaching of the cross is
foolishness (1 Cor. 1:18). How sad when the latter
profess to be one with the former!

"Whose god is their belly." Their principle aim is the
gratification of their own pleasures and the pampering
of their own appetites. "For they that are such serve not
our Lord Jesus Christ, but their own belly; and by good
words and fair speeches deceive the hearts of the simple"
(Romans 16:18).

There are more gluttons who make gods of their stom-
achs than will admit it. There is more truth than
fiction in the saying, "We dig our graves with our teeth."
That which contributes to the gratification of the flesh,

whether in what we eat or what we wear, means more to some professing Christians than anything else in their life. Herring says: "The golden calf has been cast into a different form today." One look at our gorging, our garments, and our gadgets and a voice says: "These be thy gods" (Exodus 32:4).

"Whose glory is in their shame." The heart of man must have something in which to glory, and if a man does not know Jesus Christ so as to glory in Christ's Cross, as did Paul, he will glory in the very things of which he should be ashamed. Such moral corruption, like cancer, has the strong quality of spreading. We Christians need to exercise much care lest we get our eyes upon this type of professing Christian and thereby follow a bad example. The underworld characters are not all in the slums of our cities, for here Paul pictures some in the local assembly.

"Who mind earthly things." They name Christ's Name and call themselves His, but they show by what their minds are set upon that they are His enemies. "The friendship of the world is enmity with God" (James 4:4). The true child of God wants no more of it than his Saviour had when He was here on earth. Our Lord's was no earth-bound life. Christ was no materialist. All earthly pursuits and possessions we see within our reach must have as a sound basis spiritual motives and heavenly ideals. Christian, ours is the upward calling of God in Christ Jesus (3:14). Therefore, "Set your affection on things above, not on things on the earth" (Col 3:2).

Now in contrast to the earth-mindedness of mere professors, Paul sets forth the hope and heaven-mindedness of the saints in the closing two verses of our chapter.

D. *Expectation*

For our conversation is in heaven; from whence also we look for the Saviour, the Lord Jesus Christ:

Who shall change our vile body, that it may be fashioned like unto His glorious body, according to the working whereby He is able even to subdue all things unto Himself.
Phil. 3:20-21

The apostle here presents the heavenly citizenship of the Christian believer. The word "conversation" should read "citizenship" or "commonwealth." It is from the same Greek word used in 1:27. The commonwealth of which Christians are citizens has its permanent location in Heaven. Beloved, we belong to another country, even "a city which hath foundations, whose builder and maker is God" (Heb. 11:10). You see, our expectation is from the Lord. We are but temporary pilgrims passing through this earthly vale of sorrow and death. This is one of God's ways of encouraging our hearts. We are Heaven-born, hence Heaven-bound. Do you find it difficult at times to divorce your thoughts from the material world about you? If you do, there is the possibility that Heaven has had no place in your thinking because you are not one of its citizens. The enemy of the Cross builds his metropolis down here, but the Christian's is up there.

Why does the apostle apply this terminology? Is it merely to give us an expectant hope for the future? No, not merely that! In addition to that, he would show us our responsibilities now as citizens of Heaven. One reason why the world is as bad as it is, is that some Christians are such poor citizens of Heaven. Our conduct as believers should be in agreement with our citizenship. "Now therefore ye are no more strangers and foreigners, but fellowcitizens with the saints, and of the household of God" (Eph 2:19).

We are to be a pattern of the heavenly for earth-minded people. Our heavenly citizenship does not commence at death, nor at the Rapture, but is a present reality in this world. We are expected to live by Heaven's principles and ideals now. Our civic status on earth should be as those whose home is in Heaven. Our earthly practice and walk are according to a standard far above that of earth-men. "It is because we are dropping the truths of eternity and immortality and Heaven out of our thinking that we are fast becoming a generation of earth-bound pagans." Heaven is our Father's abode; many of our loved ones are there, our interests are there, and our Saviour is there.

"From whence also we look for the Saviour, the Lord Jesus Christ." Our Lord is in Heaven, and from there we look expectantly to see Him descend. "For the Lord Himself shall descend from heaven with a shout, with the voice of the archangel, and with the trump of God: and the dead in Christ shall rise first" (1 Thess. 4:16).

We are exhorted to look for His Coming. "Looking for that blessed hope, and the glorious appearing of the great God and our Saviour Jesus Christ" (Titus 2:13).

The greatest event in any country on earth is a visit from its chief emperor. History records the most elaborate preparations and memorials for such an event. Special coins have been minted, commemorative stamps issued, and highways built. Looking forward to the Coming of our Lord Jesus Christ is the highlight of Christian expectation. We should be dwelling daily in this thought of His return. He said He was coming back (John 14:1-3).

The last words the disciples heard as He was taken up into Heaven was the testimony that He would come back again in like manner, that is, in a cloud even as He was received up (Acts 1:9-11). The saints at Corinth were exhorted to maintain a spirit of waiting for His coming (1 Cor. 1:7). It was this very spirit that the Thessalonians manifested (1 Thess. 1:10). This is our blessed hope.

The coming One is not only a "Saviour," but *"The* Saviour." There is no other. He alone is our Hope (Titus 2:13). It ill becomes a citizen of Heaven to go from day to day, and even from year to year, with little or no interest in the Second Coming of our Lord Jesus Christ. Imagine how the residents in your neighborhood would feel if the President of the United States had announced that he was making a personal appearance in your community. I feel certain there would be some special preparations for his coming. Beloved brethren, our Lord is coming again, and no twisting of words can make His Coming to mean our going to Him. As citizens of Heaven we have a right to look for Him, and when He appears He will deliver us completely and finally from all of the power and prospects of sin. The same Saviour who delivered us from the penalty of sin at His first Coming will deliver us from the presence of sin at His Second Coming. It is for His appearance we are looking and longing. Blessed be His Name!

"Who shall change our vile body, that it may be fashioned like unto His glorious body, according to the working whereby He is able to subdue all things unto Himself" (3:21). Here the Revised Version should be consulted. It reads: "Who shall fashion anew the body of

our humiliation." Our present bodies are not in condition
for their future state. In this present low estate the body
is subject to sin, suffering, and numerous other indig-
nities. The believer's body will be fashioned anew at the
Rapture of the Church when "we shall all be changed"
and "this corruptible must put on incorruption, and this
mortal must put on immortality" (1 Cor. 15:51-53). The
sin principle now resident in our bodies will not be present
then (Romans 7:17-18). These physical bodies are of
humble origin, "of the earth, earthy" (1 Cor. 15:47), of
the "dust" (Gen. 2:7), but the fall of Adam humiliated
the human body to its present low estate.

But the body of the Christian has a glorious destiny.
It is called by Paul "the redemption of our body"
(Romans 8:23). "We know that, when He shall appear,
we shall be like Him" (1 John 3:2).

Our glorified body, having undergone complete and
final redemption, will be "conformed to the body of His
glory." When our Lord came forth from the grave in
resurrection He was manifested to His disciples in a
transformed body. Though the doors were shut where
the disciples were assembled for fear of the Jews, Jesus
appeared to them in His transformed body (John 20:19).
His resurrection body was not bound by time, space, nor
substance. It was no longer subject to those laws by which
the natural body is now controlled. Millions of bodies
of the saints are at this very moment suffering from the
effects of mortality, but the moment will come when He
will redeem them all from the power of sin, sickness,
death, and the grave. Then, being like Christ's body, in
substance and nature, these earthly limitations will never
again be known. We have little control over our present

body with its mortal existence, broken by sin, but we know that our Lord will surely come and finish His work which includes the glorious destiny and exalted position of the bodies of the redeemed. Peter, James, and John caught a glimpse of the glorified body when they saw Jesus transfigured before them on the Holy Mount. Such a transformation awaits us.

Such a change will be a miracle of divine omnipotence "according to the working whereby He is able even to subdue all things unto Himself." He will do it according to the energy of His power. We saw that power in action in Christ's healing the sick and raising the dead, and we may be certain that the same divine energy, which is always a power at work, will stop at nothing when the hour of His appearing comes. No other power will be able to restrain Him since He is able to subject all things unto Himself. The change is coming; it must come, before we enter finally into our eternal home. If it seems to us that the change will be more difficult to make in some than in others, we can rest in the fact that "He is able." The joints of one body may be crippled and disarranged by some disease, still *He is able* to set each member in its proper place. He will set the whole house in order. Then He will exercise "the exceeding greatness of His power" (Eph. 1:19).

Beloved Christian, this expectation is not beyond realization: He is able. Our Lord is ready to meet any and every extremity. He will overthrow all opposition, and His grace to sinners will ultimately triumph. Rejoice in the bright and blessed expectation that is yours.

XVIII. PROBLEMS

Therefore, my brethren dearly beloved and longed for, my joy and crown, so stand fast in the Lord, my dearly beloved.

I beseech Euodias, and beseech Syntyche, that they be of the same mind in the Lord.

And I entreat thee also, true yokefellow, help those women which laboured with me in the gospel, with Clement also, and with other my fellowlabourers, whose names are in the book of life.

Rejoice in the Lord alway: and again I say, Rejoice.

Philippians 4:1-4

The exhortations that follow in the first nine verses of chapter four grow out of the aforementioned facts. The "therefore" is characteristic of Paul's method or way of relating that which has gone before. In view of the presence of enemies of the Cross of Christ, our heavenly citizenship, and the fact that we are looking for the Lord Jesus to come from Heaven—"Therefore . . . stand fast in the Lord . . . be of the same mind in the Lord . . . help those women . . . rejoice in the Lord." I see in these four exhortations, or rather this fourfold exhortation, some problems existing in the assembly in Philippi at the time of the writing of Paul's Epistle to the believers there.

The previous chapter concluded with the reminder of the all-sufficiency of the power of God to meet any and every emergency in this life as well as to effect the complete and final change of our bodies in preparation for the life which is to come. Apparently there had arisen in the Philippian church some problems which had so far baffled solution. Paul now reminds them that the same power is available to solve every problem and settle every situation in their midst. He wants them to know that nothing is beyond the power of God, hence the "therefore." The "therefore" forges a link between God's power and man's problems.

A. *The Problem of Defeatism*

Therefore, my brethren dearly beloved and longed for, my joy and crown, so stand fast in the Lord, my dearly beloved.
Phil. 4:1

Paul's exhortation indicates that they were inclined to yield ground; they were prone to retreat from a firm stand for Christ. The pressure of that pagan city tempted them to give way. No matter the situation, they are to stand unwaveringly for God and His cause. This problem of defeatism and instability has plagued the Church since its inception. We are engaged in a great spiritual conflict which calls for facing the foe without flinching. After we have put on the whole armor of God and have taken our place in the battle, we are to "withstand . . . stand . . . stand" (Eph. 6:13, 14). Some saints are too unsteady and too easily moved, but a true citizen is not quick to surrender.

The one position for power, in order to remain stead-fast, is *"in the Lord."* Unless we have learned that He is the secret of our strength and security, we will be forced to fall back in defeat. No less than eight times Paul makes use of the expression "in the Lord" (1:14; 2:19, 24, 29; 3:1; 4:1, 2, 4). You are in Christ. He is your power

Problems (4:1-4)   213

and protection; therefore stand fast in Him. You are His possession; He owns you. Therefore stand fast in Him. Stand fast in the *faith* that is in Christ (1 Cor. 16:13). Stand fast in the *fellowship* that is in Christ (Phil. 1:27). Stand fast in the *freedom* that is in Christ (Gal. 5:1). Stand fast in the *foundations* that are in Christ (2 Thess. 2:15). Here the believer is exhorted to stand fast in the *family* that is in Christ—"My brethren dearly beloved . . . stand fast in the Lord" (Phil. 4:1).

Here Paul uses terms of warm affection and true-hearted endearment. To him they are "brethren dearly beloved." They are his "brethren" since they are in one family, possessing divine life. They are dearly beloved since they are maturated by one force, divine love. This is something deeper than a philanthropic feeling for each other. Their hearts had been infused with the love of God; hence it matters much whether or not he shall ever see them again. They are fervently "longed for." Since all are members of one family and are motivated by one force, all are loved with the same love and therefore all ought to love one another. To realize this kindred relationship and reciprocity would help them to stand fast and not give way.

"My joy and crown." There was present joy in view of the prospective crown. Paul has a crown coming to him. Do you? It is the crown to be awarded to Christ's faithful witnesses for others they have won to Him. It is sometimes called the soul-winner's crown. The *stephanos*, or victor's crown, is the symbol of triumph, and it will await all those whose prayers, personal work, and sacrificial giving were instrumental in bringing others to the Saviour. These were his children in the faith and they

gave him cause for much rejoicing. "For what is our hope, or joy, or crown of rejoicing? Are not even ye in the presence of our Lord Jesus Christ at His coming?" (1 Thess. 2:19).

When, as Christ's servants, we stand before His Judgment Seat, that which will give us much joy will be the presence of those who were saved through our lives and labors as we passed through this earthly scene. "He that goeth forth and weepeth, bearing precious seed, shall doubtless come again with rejoicing, bringing his sheaves with him" (Psalm 126:6).

B. *The Problem of Disunity*

I beseech Euodias, and beseech Syntyche, that they be of the same mind in the Lord.

Phil. 4:2

Euodias and Syntyche were among those women who played a prominent part in the assembly at Philippi. We recall that it was at a women's prayer meeting where Paul first preached upon his arrival and where the Lord opened Lydia's heart to receive the gospel (Acts 16:12-15). Any pastor who is blessed with faithful, praying women in the assembly is thankful to God for them. What a blessing some sisters in Christ can be! I have often wondered how I would have managed without the godly women raised up of the Lord, who filled their places quietly without quibbling and quarreling.

But two of those women at Philippi had a falling out. They were two good women who had shown a remarkable spirit of cooperation and teamwork in the gospel with Paul. Euodias and Syntyche are nowhere else mentioned in Scripture, and what it was that caused the disunity we are not told. The pity is that Satan got an advantage over them and they became the gazingstock of those without the church. Each thought she was right and neither would take the first step to make up.

Special admonitions are now directed by Paul to each of them. He urges each to pursue the right course of conduct. Apparently the disagreement was known in the church at Philippi, else Paul would not have dealt with the matter publicly. But the spiritually-minded apostle will not take sides. He says: "I exhort Euodias, and I exhort Syntyche" (R. V.). He urges them to set aside their differences and "be of the same mind in the Lord." He is not telling them they must think alike in everything and see eye to eye on every issue. There is always room for difference of opinion and originality of thought due in part to one's environment, education, and influences. But how then can they be of one mind? Of course, such a condition could only come to pass if they come together "in the Lord." There may be diversity without division, a difference of methods without a disunity of minds, disagreement without departure. Individual subjection to Christ and His Word will save the brethren from dissension and division. Diversity can be a good thing, but disunity will destroy a testimony for Christ. Beware! And remember, there is but one way to settle any disagreement; the right way is "in the Lord."

I am making no attempt to identify the persons referred to in verse 3 lest I lead you from the point of the passage. The important thing to get hold of is the apostle's appeal to others in the church to cooperate in bringing to pass a reconciliation of Euodias and Syntyche. These two women needed help in restoring harmony. It is very often through the wise direction of some Spirit-filled man of God that dislocated saints are restored to fellowship with God and to usefulness in His service. It is our business to safeguard our Lord's interests by not allowing differences between brethren to deepen into strife and separation. The churches need more yokefellows, Christians who pull well in a double harness. "Brethren, if a man be overtaken in a fault, ye which are spiritual, restore such an one in the spirit of meekness; considering thyself, lest thou also be tempted" (Gal. 6:1).

C. *The Problem of Depression*

Rejoice in the Lord alway; and again I say, Rejoice.

Phil. 4:4

From this verse I have concluded that the spirits of the saints were running low. They were cast down, disheartened, depressed. How easily we become discouraged! And how refreshing to meet a brother or a sister in Christ who rejoices everywhere and under all circumstances. Too frequently our circumstances determine the extent and expression of joy. The division and disunity in the church had robbed those believers of their joy, as is so often the case. When we permit ourselves to stray on unholy paths we cannot be joyful.

We have stated before that this is peculiarly the Epistle of joy, the words "rejoice" and "joy" occurring numerous times throughout the four chapters. Joy is a fruit of the Spirit (Gal. 5:22), and it shines forth from every Spirit-filled Christian. Some professing Christians have given false impressions of Christianity by their somber spirits and dolefulness. The Christian life is a fountain of joy, and each of us must guard against the numerous agitations that would cause us to be cast down. "This joyous spirit is to be maintained at all times and in all circumstances, for any lapse from it weakens our defences against a settled state of depression" (J. H. Pickford). When the source of our rejoicing is "in the Lord" we can say: "Although the fig tree shall not blossom, neither shall fruit be in the vines; the labour of the olive shall fail, and the fields shall yield no meat; the flock shall be cut off from the fold, and there shall be no herd in the stalls: Yet I will rejoice in the Lord, I will joy in the God of my salvation" (Habakkuk 3:17-18).

Habakkuk rejoiced in spite of the *famine*. The meek rejoice in the face of *forbearing:* "The meek also shall increase their joy in the Lord, and the poor among men shall rejoice in the Holy One of Israel" (Isaiah 29:19).

Believers rejoice when facing their *foes:* "Behold, I will make thee a new sharp threshing instrument having teeth: thou shalt thresh the mountains, and beat them small, and shalt make the hills as chaff. Thou shalt fan them, and the wind shall carry them away, and the whirlwind shall scatter them: and thou shalt rejoice in the Lord, and shalt glory in the Holy One of Israel" (Isaiah 41:15-16).

Observe that in each instance the rejoicing is "in the Lord." If we have lost all that pertains to this life we can still rejoice in Him since He is the source of all gladness and joy.

It is an interesting observation that here the exhortation to rejoice is associated with the exhortation to quarreling saints to settle their differences. Christians are not rejoicing when they are in disagreement with one another. Disunity is a destroyer of joy. To cultivate

Christian joy so that we rejoice continually is so important that it should engage our earnest attention at all times. The Christian who is in fellowship with his Lord, as well as with other believers, does not need to stop first and count his money before he can rejoice. If we cannot rejoice in our circumstances nor in our environment, we can rejoice in the Lord. He is always cause for joy to those who love Him. Joy is the outgrowth of love. "The fruit of the Spirit is love, joy" (Gal. 5:22). Love the Lord and you will rejoice. Love the brethren and you will rejoice. Love your enemies and you will rejoice. The secret of perennial joy is in the realized fellowship with Christ and His own.

XIX. PEACE

Let your moderation be known unto all men. The Lord is at hand.

Be careful for nothing; but in every thing by prayer and supplication with thanksgiving let your requests be made known unto God.

And the peace of God, which passeth all understanding, shall keep your hearts and minds through Christ Jesus.

Finally, brethren, whatsoever things are true, whatsoever things are honest, whatsoever things are of good report; if there be any virtue, and if there be any praise, think on these things.

Those things, which ye have both learned and received, and heard, and seen in me, do: and the God of peace shall be with you.

Philippians 4:5-9

This section before us, which deals with peace, follows naturally the preceding one which takes up the matter of problems. In the assembly there were the problems of defeatism, disunity, and depression. All of this had robbed the saints of the desired peace. The apostle coveted for those dear ones in Christ the experiential knowledge of the protection of the peace of God (verse 7) and the presence of the God of peace (verse 9); thus he proceeds to set forth the secret to a life of peace of mind and true happiness of heart.

A. *Requisites for Peace*

Let your moderation be known unto all men. The Lord is at hand.

Phil. 4:5

The Revised Version translates "moderation" to read *"forbearance."* Others have rendered the same word *yieldingness, gentleness, considerateness, sweet reasonableness, agreeableness, pliability,* and *courtesy.* In any of these words one finds the opposite of obstinacy and self-will.

Banish all thought that the word "moderation" here can be used as a cloak to cover sin. Our present usage of this term, we are told, permits a moderate indulgence in certain practices common to our times. For instance, a certain tobacco company displays the following: "Moderate Smokers Prefer————Cigarettes." A liquor concern peddles its poison with the following advertisement: "If you drink moderately you'll enjoy————whiskey." These things do not call for moderation but for complete eradication, for total abstinence.

There is a much broader and deeper meaning given to the word. There was disunity between Euodias and Syntyche because one was determined to have her way; one insisted upon her right; one would not yield ground. Think not at all that the apostle is calling upon anyone to sacrifice right principles. But rather, for the sake of peace, he asks us to be ready to yield that which we call our rights, our position, our preference. He is pleading for a mildness of disposition whose noble impulses of gentleness and yieldingness urge the grace of giving up. This sweet reasonableness is to find expression in our conduct toward others, that is, we are to "let it be known unto all men." No exhortation could have better met the needs of those in Philippi who were at variance with each other. Sweet reasonableness subdues explosive tempers and stubborn wills and avoids extremes in such a way that everyone with whom we come in contact will observe the condition.

But someone will say: "If I yield, and do not stand up for my rights, I may be a loser." So what? Read on, for Paul adds: "The Lord is at hand." This may be taken to mean that the Lord is near and He will provide for His own. Or it may mean that He is coming again personally and will recompense in that day for all you have forfeited through your gentleness and courtesy here. But I rather like to think of this statement as referring to His nearness now in every circumstance. He said: "Lo, I am with you alway, even unto the end of the world [consummation of the age]" (Matt. 28:20).

How assuring to know that the Lord is standing by and that He will never suffer His own to be a loser! Fear and worry over the loss of prestige, position, or even our possessions disappear with the awareness that the One who loves us and provides for us is present. He is here now in the Person of the Holy Spirit to give us grace and power for the present, and He will come again to reward us for faithfulness to Him and His Word. "The Lord is nigh unto all them that call upon Him, to all that call upon Him in truth" (Psalm 145:18).

The second requisite for peace follows:

> Be careful for nothing; but in every thing by prayer and supplication with thanksgiving let your requests be made known unto God.
>
> Phil. 4:6

The word "carefull" connotes the idea of anxiety. Paul is saying: "In nothing be anxious." There is a fretful anxiety about material things that is robbing not a few Christians of that desired peace of mind. Like Martha we are "careful [anxious] . . . about many things" (Luke 10:41), when we should be "careful [anxious] for nothing." In Matthew 6:24-34 our Lord taught His disciples the need for daily dependence upon their Heavenly Father. He urges them to "take no thought," that is, they are not to become anxious about food, drink, clothing, shelter, or their earthly future. Such fretful anxiety prevents the Word of God from taking root in our lives because the care of this world chokes the Word and we become unfruitful (Matt. 13:7, 22). Our needs are God's concern and thus they are His care and responsibility. "Casting all your care upon Him; for He careth for you" (1 Peter 5:7). "Let your conversation [manner of life] be without covetousness [fondness for money and things]; and be content with such things as ye have: for He hath said, I will never leave thee, nor forsake thee" (Heb. 13:5).

Are *you* given to worry? The Philippian Christians were continuously worrying, and Paul exhorted them to stop it. To worry is to sin, and here is one sin, like all others, that will rob the heart and mind of peace. We may encounter trials and troubles but it is wrong to brood over them. Such anxiety distracts our minds from Christ and His Words, thereby preventing spiritual growth. We are warned to take heed lest our Lord come and find our hearts overcharged with the "cares of this life" (Luke 21:34). It is possible to be cautious and rightly concerned, and yet not be anxious. Now quit your worrying, for "Worry is the interest we pay on the debt of unbelief with which we have mortgaged life." Faith ends where anxiety begins, so never give way to anxiety.

The requisite for peace continues:

> But in every thing by prayer and supplication with thanksgiving let your requests be made known unto God.
>
> Phil. 4:6

Keep in mind that we are still looking at a part of the same sentence in which Paul says, "Be careful for nothing." How utterly incomplete, to say the least, is this exhortation if it must stand alone. But Paul does not say, "Be careful for nothing," and then stop there. He adds the positive approach to the solution of our problems: namely, we are to come to God in prayer and bring Him into every difficulty and deficiency in our lives. Here is the secret of a carefree life—careful for nothing but prayerful for everything.

Observe that we are to pray about *everything*—"in every thing by prayer. . . ." Think not at all that God is not interested in the small and insignificant things that worry you and me. What a privilege to carry *everything* to God in prayer. Our Heavenly Father is interested in every detail of our lives, therefore come boldly unto His throne of grace and open your heart to Him. God delights to hear His children tell Him "everything." He tells us not to be careful but prayerful. Do not reduce the Infinite to the finite by placing a limit on Him. He would have us confide the minutest detail in Him. Nothing is too small, nothing is too large, to bring to Him in prayer.

"And supplication." The word for "prayer" *(proseuché)* is used for prayer in general as an act of devotion and worship. The word for "supplication" *(deésis)* is used for some special petition. Here is urgent prayer for some particular need.

"With thanksgiving." Our prayers and petitions must be mingled with praise. No matter how great a need might appear in our eyes, we ever have something for which to be thankful. And remember, the sincere praise of our hearts is ever acceptable to God. Turn your cares to prayers and your problems to praise. Prayer and supplication *with thanksgiving* springs from a deeper sense of the goodness and mercy of the Lord. In the hour of need examine the credit side of the ledger and your heart will cry with the Psalmist: "Bless the Lord, O my soul, and forget not all his benefits" (Psalm 103:2).

A necessary element of true prayer is thankfulness for past blessings. "Careful for nothing . . . prayerful for everything . . . thankful for anything" (Guy H. King).

B. *Results of Peace*

And the peace of God, which passeth all understanding, shall keep your hearts and minds through Christ Jesus.

Phil. 4:7

In one sense we could say that peace is the result of prayer since prayer always brings peace. When the heart is in a prayer relation to God it knows perfect peace, *"the peace of God."* In exchange for our problems He gives us His peace. It is a peace *"which passeth all understanding."* Now a peace possessed by one who has health, wealth, friends, and loved ones, is quite understandable, but the peace of God in the midst of trial and tribulation is something far different. Jesus said: "Peace I leave with you, My peace I give unto you: not as the world giveth, give I unto you. Let not your heart be troubled, neither let it be afraid" (John 14:27).

His peace is a legacy bequeathed, "not as the world

giveth." This world system demands a price for peace but it cannot deliver the goods after the price has been paid. The price for the peace of God has been paid for us, for Christ "made peace through the blood of His cross" (Col. 1:20). In His last will and testament our blessed Lord made the legacy available to us. Now all who receive Him can enjoy harmonized relations with God. I do not possess the faculty to perceive it all, since it passeth all understanding, but though I cannot perceive it, I may receive it; and so may you.

The peace of God acts as a guard, or sentinel, at the door of the heart and mind. Paul said that it *"shall keep* [or garrison] *your hearts and minds through Christ Jesus."* When we dwell upon our problems and perplexities, our hearts and minds become seriously affected, so much so that we go all to pieces. This is Satan's strong point of attack and I fear he has succeeded in making neurotics of great numbers of professing Christians. But God's peace does sentinel duty over our hearts and minds to prevent any successful attack on the part of the enemy. God's peace is a priceless commodity that this old world cannot purchase with money, nor can it be had through the efforts of modern psychiatry. "Careful for nothing . . . prayerful for everything . . . thankful for anything"— this is the secret! When everything is placed trustingly into the hands of our Heavenly Father in prayer, petition, and praise, we know that He will keep watch over our hearts and minds so that nothing can upset us mentally or emotionally.

C. *Replacements of Peace*

Finally, brethren, whatsoever things are true, whatsoever

things are honest, whatsoever things are just, whatsoever things are pure, whatsoever things are lovely, whatsoever things are of good report; if there be any virtue and if there be any praise, think on these things.

Phil. 4:8

In verse 6 we have those things of which we must rid our minds: namely, anxious thoughts. Here we have the things that are to occupy the mind as a replacement.

"Whatsoever things are *true*." The mind must have something with which to occupy itself. Here we are told to exercise the thought-life with the genuine, the sincere, the simple. A sound rule of mental health is to be genuinely and sincerely true to God, true to our fellowmen, and true to our responsibilities.

"Whatsoever things are *honest*." We are to give thought to those things that are honorable, grave, and venerable, and that claim respect.

"Whatsoever things are *just*." Thought must be given to that which is right or righteous, both by divine and human standards.

"Whatosever things are *pure*." Purity in all things must be a part of one's thought-life. The peace of God will replace wrong thoughts, with pure thoughts, impure motives with pure motives, and impure acts with pure acts.

"Whatsoever things are *lovely*." Beauty of character is a worthly replacement for the ugly, the selfish, and the arrogant. The former draws while the latter repels. That which is lovely shows forth the beauty of holiness.

"Whatsover things are *of good report*." The good report is the well-sounding well-spoken report that wins the approbation of others.

Concerning these six virtues, Paul says: *"Think on these things."* These are things that call for careful reflection. Our minds should dwell on them at all times. Have you examined your thought-life of late? It is an easy matter for one's mind to become sluggish and lax, thereby giving thought to those things that would rob us of peace. It has been said that you cannot prevent a bird from flying over your head, but you can prevent it from building a nest in your hair. So it is with wrong thoughts. By thinking positively on "these things" we will crowd out those things of ill repute that only tend to disturb the mind.

> Those things, which ye have both learned, and received, and heard, and seen in me, do: and the God of Peace shall be with you.
>
> Phil. 4:9

The Philippian assembly had learned and received and heard many great truths from Paul while he was with them. Moreover, he was an example by his own life of what he taught. Those things he now exhorts them to "do." They are not merely to "think" upon those virtues mentioned in verse 8; they are to "do" them, even as they had been expounded and exemplified before them. They are to behave them as well as to believe them. Paul's doctrine and his deportment were in unison. He could write: "But thou hast fully known my doctrine, manner of life" (2 Tim. 3:10).

Paul preached what he practiced. Truth reads well and sounds beautiful, but it is not something merely to be written down for one to read and admire. We have not learned "those things" until we have lived them.

"If ye know these things, happy are ye if ye do them" (John 13:17).

Noble thoughts are of little value unless they are translated into deeds. Living surpasses learning; practice outshines preaching; living supersedes learning. As we conform to orthodox thinking in our daily living, we have the sweet assurance that "the God of peace shall be with you." In verse 7 we have "the peace of God" and in verse 9 "the God of peace." Both the power of the peace of God and the presence of the God of peace are the portion of those who obey the truth. What a happy, contented people we should be!

XX. PROVISION

But I rejoiced in the Lord greatly, that now at the last your care of me hath flourished again; wherein ye were also careful, but ye lacked opportunity.

Not that I speak in respect of want: for I have learned, in whatsoever state I am, therewith to be content.

I know both how to be abased, and I know how to abound: every where and in all things I am instructed both to be full and to be hungry, both to abound and to suffer need.

I can do all things through Christ which strengtheneth me.

Notwithstanding ye have well done, that ye did communicate with my affliction.

Now ye Philippians know also, that in the beginning of the gospel, when I departed from Macedonia, no church communicated with me as concerning giving and receiving, but ye only.

For even in Thessalonica ye sent once and again unto my necessity.

Not because I desire a gift: but I desire fruit that may abound to your account.

But I have all, and abound: I am full, having received of Epaphroditus the things which were sent from you, an odour of a sweet smell, a sacrifice acceptable, wellpleasing to God.

But my God shall supply all your need according to His riches in glory by Christ Jesus.

Philippians 4:10-19

Having just concluded the abiding requisites for peace and having urged upon the saints those things that should occupy their minds, the apostle now tells them how wondrously God has provided for him in every way. He recognizes, and rejoices in, the divine provision for his material, mental, and spiritual needs.

A. *Provision of Substance*

But I rejoiced in the Lord greatly, that now at the last your care of me hath flourished again; wherein ye were also careful, but ye lacked opportunity.

Phil. 4:10

Earlier he exhorted them to "rejoice in the Lord." Now he testifies, "I rejoiced in the Lord." When Paul was among them, possibly ten or twelve years before the writing of this Epistle, they ministered to his needs. Then, for some reason either not known or not given, they "lacked opportunity" to minister to those needs of God's servant. But now Epaphroditus has brought to Paul a love offering from those very saints at Philippi, so that Paul writes, "your care of me hath flourished again." Their gift was as a revival of the buds and blossoms at springtime. He received their selfless expression of love as a thing of beauty. While he was sitting in the Roman prison, his needs were few, so he testified:

But I have all, and abound: I am full, having received of Epaphroditus the things which were sent from you, an odour of a sweet smell, a sacrifice acceptable, wellpleasing to God.
Phil. 4:18

The gifts they sent more than met his needs, and he looked upon them as a fragrant and acceptable offering which is pleasing to God. Any gift, whether to the Lord's work or to the Lord's workmen, is of greater worth and higher significance when viewed as a gift to God. The burnt offerings that went up from the altar ascended as "a sweet savour unto the Lord" (Lev. 1:9), thereby signifying that with the offerings Jehovah was well pleased. (See also Genesis 8:20-22.) Paul also wrote of our Lord: "And walk in love, as Christ also hath loved us, and hath given Himself for us an offering and a sacrifice to God for a sweetsmelling savour" (Eph. 5:2).

Christ offered Himself a sacrifice *for* us but His death was "an offering and a sacrifice *to* God." His death was costly and was therefore worth much to God. Now it is the same word that Paul uses of the offering of the Philippian saints. However much or little it was, God accepted it as a sweet savour offering. It was evidently a sacrifice on their part, and with that kind of giving God is pleased.

Right here we can learn a worthful lesson. If we give only sparingly out of our abundance, whether of time, money, or strength in service, our giving does not ascend to Heaven as a sacrifice pleasing unto the Lord. God delights to receive from His people a sacrifice motivated by a loving and willing heart. The Philippians had collected money and sent it to Rome to help God's servant in need. Paul accepted this provision of substance as coming from the Lord, inasmuch as they had given it to the Lord. Their gifts were well-pleasing because they were given sacrificially and cheerfully when others were not giving at all.

> Now ye Philippians know also, that in the beginning of the gospel, when I departed from Macedonia, no church communicated with me as concerning giving and receiving, but ye only.
> For even in Thessalonica ye sent once and again unto my necessity.
>
> Phil. 4:15, 16

In recalling their former gifts Paul confirms his faith

in the motive of their giving. His heart is full of emotion and appreciation since through them God had provided the substance whereby he could carry on in the gospel ministry. Now he is rejoicing for their sakes since he has their deepest interests at heart. He knew that giving is an integral and essential part of every believer's spiritual life, and that there are rewards awaiting all who grow in grace. He adds:

> Not because I desire a gift: but I desire fruit that may abound to your account.
>
> Phil. 4:17

He had enough for his needs. God had seen to that. But now he desires that they might reap the reward of giving in the life to come. The grace and glory of spiritual giving is a virtue that adorns too few of us. The churches in Macedonia were an excellent example of growth in the grace of giving. "Moreover, brethren, we do you to wit of the grace of God bestowed on the churches of Macedonia; How that in a great trial of affliction the abundance of their joy and their deep poverty abounded unto the riches of their liberality. . . . And this they did, not as we hoped, but first gave their own selves to the Lord, and unto us by the will of God. Insomuch that we desired Titus, that as He had begun, so He would also finish in you the same grace also" (2 Cor. 8:1-2, 5, 6).

They gave largely because they were growing in grace and in the knowledge of our Lord Jesus Christ (2 Pet. 3:18). "For ye know the grace of our Lord Jesus Christ, that, though He was rich, yet for your sakes He became poor, that ye through His poverty might be rich" (2 Cor. 8:9).

Christ did not give sparingly of Himself but bountifully. He was grace personified; therefore He gave graciously, freely, and willingly of His substance and His own self. The incentive in giving is not the compulsion of a law, but the constraint of love. Christian giving does not reach its climax with a tithe since the Christian gives apart from the law. Our giving is not law-giving but grace-giving. Christ is our supreme Example. Being rich, He voluntarily became poor that we might be made rich through His poverty. Thus He did not think of giving in terms of duty but in terms of bounty. The more bountifully we sow, the more bountifully we reap, since what is given is not a contribution but an investment. "But this I say, He which soweth sparingly shall reap also sparingly; and he which soweth bountifully shall reap also bountifully. Every man according as he purposeth in his heart, so let him give; not grudgingly, or of necessity: for God loveth a cheerful giver" (2 Cor. 9:6, 7).

B. *Provision of Satisfaction*

Not that I speak in respect of want: for I have learned, in whatever state I am, therewith to be content.

Phil. 4:11

Usually we seek and find contentment in the possession of things, believing that those things we desire will make us content. But we discover after a while that contentment based upon our position and possessions is an elusive objective always beyond our reach. The contentment that Paul speaks about here is dependent upon Christ. It is "in the Lord." The rise and fall of the dollar value left Paul undisturbed. Chained in a prison cell was not an experience that could spoil his contentment. Earthly position and possessions add nothing to and subtract nothing from the real satisfaction to be found in Jesus Christ. It is an inner satisfaction which enables the trusting child of God to live above external conditions and circumstances. "Take heed, and beware of covetousness: for a man's life consisteth not in the abundance of the things he possesseth" (Luke 12:15). "And having food and raiment let us be therewith content" (1 Tim. 6:8).

In those early days of my Christian experience I could not see how some Christians I knew could be content with so little of this world's goods. I sincerely trust that I am learning the secret. From what I see about me I do not hesitate to say that it is a secret many Christians have yet to learn. Paul needed to learn it. He said, "I have learned. . . ." The lesson of contentment was one he learned by degrees in varying circumstances. As a young unbelieving Jew, he had no want insofar as this world's possessions are concerned. He did not always know the divine provision of satisfaction, but after he was saved he came to learn it, not in the academic classroom, but as the result of a lengthy experience of trials and discipline. "I have learned" is the language of a good student. Have you learned to be satisfied with your place and position and possessions in this life? "Let your conversation be without covetousness; and be content with such things as ye have: for He hath said, I will never leave thee, nor forsake thee" (Heb. 13:5).

Paul's satisfaction was not because of his present conditions but because of the presence of Christ. Happy is the man who learns the lesson of doing without; not that he is conceitedly self-sufficient, but that he depends upon the sufficiency of Jesus Christ. "Not that we are sufficient of ourselves to think any thing as of ourselves; but our sufficiency is of God. . . . And God is able to make all grace abound toward you, that ye, always having all sufficiency in all things, may abound to every good work" (2 Cor. 3:5; 9:8).

This provision of satisfaction which grows out of one's utter dependence upon the Lord is life's greatest asset. Paul calls it great gain. "But godliness with contentment is great gain" (1 Tim. 6:6).

Paul follows by giving us the secret to a life of contentment:

> I know both how to be abased, and I know how to abound: every where and in all things I am instructed both to be full and to be hungry, both to abound and to suffer need.
>
> Phil. 4:12

In the process of learning he discovered a secret that can be revealed only in the actual experience itself but can never become known to the uninitiated. Only as one learns to trust the sufficiency of the Saviour in the ups and downs of life can one learn the secret of a carefree and contented experience. He learned to trust Christ in the day of plenty as in the day of poverty. He looked to the Lord in thanksgiving for luxuries as well as for little. Any Christian who will commit himself into God's care, and then trust Him whether his fare be much or meager, will enjoy peace and contentment. Paul had been taught and initiated in two schools, the one in which he was provided for in an abundant way and the other where he was abased by adverse circumstances. His soul had learned the art of close communion with God regardless of his supply or his surroundings, thus he could get along on a little or a lot, but neither condition affected his inner state.

Do you have complete contentment at all times and under all circumstances? A mighty lesson to learn is this.

C. *Provision of Strength*

I can do all things through Christ which strengtheneth me.
Phil. 4:13

This is no idle boast, nor is it the voice of one telling us that he always gets his own way. Rather it is the testimony of a godly man to the power of the indwelling Christ. Knowing that no limitations can be placed on the divine dynamo, Paul is testifying that he is a match for any circumstance. He can be content independent of circumstances but he cannot be independent of Christ in any circumstance. The divine call to any task or trial is always accompanied by the divine enablement to be triumphant. But keep before you the fact that we do not conquer in our own strength. We are not wrong in acknowledging human weakness, but we are wrong when we fail to trust completely in the power of God. Whenever God requires us to do anything we must say with Paul, "I can . . . *through Christ*." "We are more than conquerors *through Him*" (Rom. 8:37).

How often have we failed in some endeavor because we attempted it in our own strength? If only we had recognized Christ's presence in us, and then trusted in Him and His power, we would have been victorious. Now I am not suggesting that we do nothing at all. Roy L. Lauren says,

"The principle expressed in this verse gives the proper place to the regenerated personality of the Christian. It neither minimizes nor magnifies the place of Christian personality. It does not teach that the Christian does everything for himself; nor does it teach that God does everything for the Christian. What this verse does teach is that there is a place for the regenerated personality as well as a responsibility. God makes us responsible to do while He becomes responsible to supply us with the strength to do. Instead of saying that Christ does everything and I do nothing, it says 'I can do all things through Christ which strengtheneth me.' The crux of the verse is 'which strengtheneth me.' "

We can rely on the Lord in all things; if only He could rely on us! We have no right to plead our weakness and poverty as an excuse to get out from under responsibility. Paul's body was overpowered, bound, and put in a prison cell by enemies of Jesus Christ, but such a circumstance did not spell defeat for Christ and His cause nor for Paul. This prison Epistle in itself is a mighty victory for the Son of God. Now, my brethren, we have Paul's Christ, and our Saviour's power avails for us as it did for Paul. The saint who is weakest in himself can be the strongest through Christ. "Therefore I take pleasure in infirmities, in reproaches, in necessities, in persecutions, in distresses for Christ's sake: for when I am weak, then am I strong" (2 Cor. 12:10).

If one is prone to wonder how Paul accomplished so much while suffering labors more abundant, stripes above measure, prisons more frequent, facing death often, beaten with rods, stoned, shipwrecked, robbed, hungry, and cold, one has the answer in his testimony, "I can do all things through Christ." The power of Christ in Paul's life was his enablement. And so it is for the life that lies ahead of you and me. Paul accomplished great things for God even though he suffered much. Fixing his eyes on the Saviour he said, "I can." And so can you and I.

But what does Paul mean by "all things"? Not all things we might like to do, but all the things we ought to do. If you have never taken lessons in flying an airplane, do not get into the cockpit and take off. I doubt very much if you would have a right to expect the Lord to give you a happy landing. I refuse to jump into water that is over my head, simply because I cannot swim. But in those things we know are required of us, we must learn to tackle them in Christ's strength. Whatever we need, we must turn to Christ for its supply, and He will be in us the Power to do and be. To the weak He is Strength; to the ignorant He is Wisdom; to those lacking courage He is their Courage; to the proud He is their Humility. Paul could be wanting for food and shelter without bitterness or complaint, but only through Christ. On the other hand he could be abounding in an oversupply of this world's goods and not be conceited or proud, but only through Christ. The ability of Christ knows no inability; why not trust Him?

D. *Provision of Supply*

But my God shall supply all your need according to His riches in glory by Christ Jesus.

Phil. 4:19

Having pointed his reader to Christ as the Provider of strength to be and do, Paul now points to Him as the One through whom the Father provides all our needs. I would guess that there is hardly a Christian anywhere who is not in some kind of need—material, mental, spiritual. The appetites of the flesh, the appeal of the world, and the attacks of the devil place us in the position of some sort of need at all times. The need for our complete and final redemption has been met in Christ, and neither time nor circumstances nor powers can alter that finished work in our behalf. But we are still subject to trials, testings, and temptations, and we still need guidance, courage, and strength. Regardless of what the need might be, Paul includes the whole sweep of human needs—"all your need" —the physical, social, intellectual, spiritual—every need.

We sometimes want things it is a thousand times better for us that we do not have. Then, too, we draw back from those things which, as a matter of fact, we really need. Too often the flesh dictates its desires and we selfishly reach out for those things we do not need and that serve no good purpose in our lives.

Looking at the text within the context, Paul has in mind the gap left in those Philippian saints because of their sacrificial giving. They could be certain that any need created because of what they gave to Christ and His cause, God would supply. We are not told the nature or size of their gift brought by Epaphroditus to Paul, but we know that it was a substantial one (verse 18). As though to balance their sacrificial giving, Paul sends them this assuring word that God would supply all their need. They had met Paul's needs for spreading the gospel; now God will fill their needs.

"Not that our giving to the Lord should be looked upon as a reciprocal trade agreement. We should not give to get; but our giving to the Lord will always insure our getting from the Lord. Nothing that we give to the Lord is overlooked. On the other hand, what grounds have we to lay hold of this promise to supply our needs if we have refused to supply the needs of God's work when we had the means? With what confidence can we pray for the Lord to honour us with substance if we have not honoured Him with the substance that He has already given? This is an ageless principle in the economy of God: what we withhold, withers, but what we scatter, gathers; what we lay aside, spoils, but what we release, returns. If we fill full another's needs, God will fill full our needs." J. H. Pickford.

The Philippians filled Paul's cup to overflowing; now they can depend upon God's filling theirs.

The *source* of the supply is suggested in the words, "my God." All earthly wealth is temporary and transient; it is passing away (1 John 2:17). Depressions wipe out whole fortunes; thieves steal an entire life's savings; time deteriorates buildings; but nothing and no one can wrest from the God of the universe the wealth that is His. He accumulated it and He allocates it. Riches are safe with Him, hence the importance of one's source. The God who created and sustains the universe has the interests of His children at heart. In all His majesty and might He is the merciful source of supply to each believer who obeys Him, so that any one of us can reckon Him as "my God." When I cannot see my way clear, *my God* shall supply; when man does not take cognizance of my needs, *my God* shall supply; when there is no other source of supply, *my God* shall supply.

The *surety* of the supply is suggested in the word "shall." Here is a note of certainty that should cast out every doubt from our minds. There is never an occasion to fear with such assurance. The Psalmist said: "The Lord is my Shepherd; I shall not want" (Psalm 23:1). He was sure of being led and fed, protected and provided for, no matter the circumstance. He was sure because of the source. If the promises of God fail, nothing is certain. But we have no need to fear; He cannot fail because of who He is. When others do not come to your rescue, He shall; when you cannot, He shall; when there seems to be no way of reaching your needs, He shall.

The *sufficiency* of the supply is suggested in the words "all your need." I fear we often fail to distinguish between our needs and our desires. The things that are needful for us are sometimes most unpleasant. Paul's desire on one occasion was that he be delivered from his thorn in the flesh, but that was not his need. His real need was for more grace, and that is what God supplied (2 Cor. 12:7-9). Nowhere has God promised to supply our wants and desires, but only our needs. Now some of our needs seem large to us, but they are all so little to Him. Knowing that there is not a single need that He will not supply will save us from despairing moments. Remember now, not all your greed, but all your need; not all your desires, but all your need; not all that you think you need, but all you need.

The *standard* of the supply is suggested in the words "according to His riches." I am unable to tell you exactly what is meant by "His riches in glory." It includes all the vast wealth of the universe, but that is a mere drop in a bucket compared with His glorious riches untold. Contextually His riches meet the needs of this present life, but they project far out into eternity. Paul knew something of His riches, for he wrote of "the riches of His goodness" (Rom. 2:4), "the riches of His wisdom" (Rom. 11:33), "the riches of His grace" (Eph. 1:7), "the riches of His glory" (Eph. 3:16). God's standard for giving is "according to," not "out of," His riches. Our standard of giving is far below God's. We give meagerly out of our abundance, not considering the need of those to whom we give nor the cause to which we give. God's standard is loftier and nobler than man's, and we should be thankful it is so.

XXI. POSTLUDE

Now unto God and our Father be glory for ever and ever.
Amen.

Salute every saint in Christ Jesus. The brethren which are
with me greet you.

All the saints salute you, chiefly they that are of Caesar's
household.

The grace of our Lord Jesus Christ be with you all. Amen.
Philippians 4: 20-23

Paul bursts forth into a note of praise to God for His
wondrous provision for His children. He knows that to
God must be the glory and he wants it to be that way
in his own thinking and ours. The glory is His and shall
be His forever and ever. "Amen." So it is and so let it
be!

After Paul glorifies God he greets the saints. Mutual
salutations are in order from the saints at Rome to the
saints at Philippi, and to all saints everywhere. The Christians at Rome had never met the Christians at Philippi,
but there was a kindred spirit between them, thus they
wished to be remembered to them. All saints are dear to
our Heavenly Father and should be dear to each other.
There should be a loving concern on our part for each
member of the Body of Christ.

Finally, Paul leaves with them, and us, a precious
thought on which to linger—"the grace of our Lord Jesus

Christ." And with this benediction Paul concludes his letter. I can hear the strains of the postlude sounding out the "glory" of the Father and the "grace" of our Lord Jesus Christ, with the final "Amen" to the Father (verse 20), and the final "Amen" to the Son (verse 23). Amen! Amen!

BIBLIOGRAPHY

ADAM, JAMES RUSSELL. *The Courier of God's Grace*. Westwood, New Jersey: Revell, 1948.

ANDERSON, HENRY E. *Outline Studies of Philippians*. London: Marshall, Morgan, and Scott.

BORLAND, ANDREW. *By This Conquer*. Kilmarnock: John Ritchie.

CASH, W. WILSON. *Helps to the Study of Philippians*. London: Church Missionary Society, 1933.

HARRISON, NORMAN B. *His in Joyous Experience*. Chicago, Illinois: B.I. C.A., 1926.

HERRING, RALPH A. *Studies in Philippians*. Nashville, Tennessee: Broadman, 1952.

HOPKINS, JOHN E. *The Psychology of Philippians*. John E. Hopkins, 1946.

IRONSIDE, H. A. *Notes on Philippians*. New York: Loizeaux Brothers, 1922.

JOHNSTONE, ROBERT. *The Epistle of Paul to the Philippians*. Grand Rapids, Michigan: Baker, 1955.

KEEN, CLARENCE M. *Paul's Letter to the Philippians*. Wilmington, Del.: 1926.

KING, GUY H. *Joy Way*. London: Marshall, Morgan, and Scott, 1952.

LAURIN, ROY L. *Life Advances*. Chicago, Illinois: Van Kampen, 1953.

LIGHTFOOT, J. B. *St. Paul's Epistle to the Philippians*. London: Macmillan and Co., 1913.

LINCOLN, WILLIAM. *The Epistle to the Philippians*. Kilmarnock: John Ritchie.

MACLAREN, ALEXANDER. *Expositions of Holy Scripture*. New York: Hodder and Stoughton.

MEYER, F. B. *The Epistle to the Philippians*. London: Religious Tract Society, 1921.

MOULE, H. C. G. *Philippian Studies*. London: Hodder and Stoughton, 1897.

MULLER, JAC. J. *The Epistles of Paul to the Philippians and to Philemon*. Grand Rapids, Michigan: Eerdmans, 1955.

NOBLE, FREDERICK A. *Discourses on Philippians.* Westwood, New Jersey: Revell, 1896.

PAYNE, STEPHEN W. *Toward the Mark.* Westwood, New Jersey: Revell, 1953.

PICKFORD, JOHN H. *Paul's Spiritual Autobiography.* London: Marshall, Morgan, and Scott, 1949.

RAINY, ROBERT. *The Epistle to the Philippians.* London: Hodder and Stoughton, 1893.

ROBERTSON, A. T. *Paul's Joy in Christ.* Westwood, New Jersey: Revell, 1917.

TENNEY, MERRILL C. *Philippians.* Grand Rapids, Michigan: Eerdmans, 1956.

TRITT, JESSIE A. *The Philippians and Paul the Apostle.* Los Angeles, Calif.: American Prophetic League.

VINE, W. E. *Epistles to the Philippians and Colossians.* London: Oliphants, 1955.

WILSON, WALTER, L. *Messages on Philippians.* Grand Rapids, Michigan: Zondervan, 1943.

WUEST, KENNETH S. *Philippians in the Greek New Testament.* Grand Rapids, Michigan: Eerdmans, 1942.

INDEX OF SCRIPTURE TEXTS